THE ART OF

MANLINESS

MANVOTIONALS

THE ART OF MANLINESS

MANVOTIONALS

TIMELESS WISDOM AND ADVICE ON LIVING THE 7 MANLY VIRTUES

BRETT AND KATE McKAY

HOW BOOKS

Cincinnati, Ohio
www.howdesign.com

For more excellent books and resources for designers, visit www.howdesign.com.

16 15 14 13 12   6 5 4 3 2

DISTRIBUTED IN CANADA BY FRASER DIRECT
100 Armstrong Avenue
Georgetown, Ontario, Canada L7G 5S4
Tel: (905) 877-4411

DISTRIBUTED IN THE U.K. AND EUROPE BY F&W MEDIA INTERNATIONAL, LTD
Brunel House, Forde Close, Newton Abbot, TQ12 4PU, UK
Tel: (+44) 1626 323200, Fax: (+44) 1626 323319
Email: enquiries@fwmedia.com

DISTRIBUTED IN AUSTRALIA BY CAPRICORN LINK
P.O. Box 704, Windsor, NSW 2756 Australia
Tel: (02) 4577-3555

Edited by **AMY OWEN**
Designed by **GRACE RING**
Cover illustration © **2011 JUPITERIMAGES**
Production coordinated by **GREG NOCK**

About the Authors

Brett McKay is a man. Kate McKay loves manly men. Together, these partners in crime run ArtofManliness.com, one of the largest men's websites on the Internet. They are also the authors of *The Art of Manliness: Classic Skills and Manners for the Modern Man*. The husband and wife team resides in Tulsa, Oklahoma, with their son Gus.

Dedication

 *To Gus*

TABLE OF CONTENTS

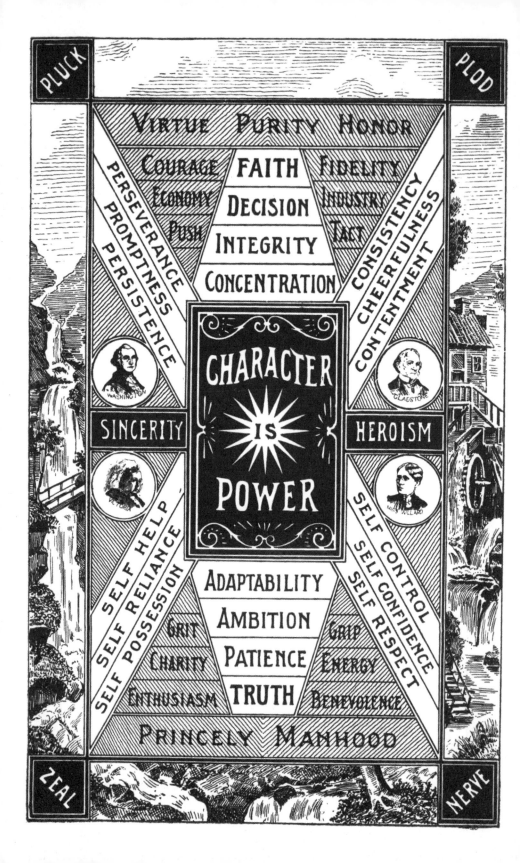

INTRODUCTION

In our first book, *The Art of Manliness: Classic Skills and Manners for the Modern Man,* we presented men with a manual that largely focused on the how-tos, the important skill sets of well-rounded manliness. The book served as a handbook of practical, manly know-how.

But the other—and even more important—side of manliness is the *mindset,* the cultivation of the inner man.

Of course it's easier to explain what a man should *do,* than what a man should *be.* To discuss the latter, we must first get at the heart of what true manliness really means.

While the definition of manliness has been endlessly discussed and dissected in scholarly tomes, our definition of manliness is actually quite straightforward. And ancient.

For the ancient Greeks, the ideal life was one filled with *eudaimonia.* What's eudaimonia? Translators and philosophers have given different definitions for it, but the best way to describe eudaimonia is the attainment of "flourishing," through, as Aristotle put it, "doing and living well." Greek philosophers believed that eudaimonia was achieved through the practice of *arete.* Translated as "virtue," arete is better understood as *excellence* and was sometimes used interchangeably with *andreia,* or "manliness." The man of arete maximized his full potential in body, mind, and soul; despite setbacks and challenges, he effectively used his abilities to fulfill his life's purpose and achieve a real and lasting legacy.

Thus for the ancient Greeks, manliness meant *being the best man you could be.*

The Latin word for manliness or masculine strength was *virtus* (this is where we get the English word "virtue"). The Roman idea of virtus at first centered on valor and courage, and later came to encompass other qualities such as fortitude, industry, and dutifulness. So for the ancient Romans, manliness meant *living a life of virtue.*

So our definition of manliness, like that of the ancients, is simple: striving for virtue, honor, and excellence in all areas of your life, fulfilling your potential as a man, and being the absolute best brother, friend, husband, father and citizen you can be.

Living a life of virtuous excellence is harder than learning how to tie a tie or start a fire, but no other pursuit will be as supremely rewarding.

At this point, some of you may be thinking, "Wait, wait, shouldn't women be striving to live the virtuous life as well?"

Absolutely.

There are two ways to define manhood. One way is to say that manhood is the opposite of *womanhood.* The other is to say that manhood is the opposite of *childhood.*

The former seems to be quite popular, but it often leads to a superficial kind of manliness. Men who subscribe to this philosophy end up cultivating a manliness concerned with *outward characteristics.* They worry about whether x, y, or z is manly and whether the things they enjoy and do are effeminate because many women also enjoy them.

We advocate the latter philosophy; *manhood* is the opposite of *childhood* and concerns one's *inner values.* A child is self-centered, fearful, and dependent. A man is bold, courageous, respectful, independent and of service to others. Thus a boy becomes a man when he matures and leaves behind childish things. Likewise, a girl becomes a woman when she matures into real adulthood.

Both genders are capable of and should strive for virtuous, human excellence. When a woman lives the virtues, that is womanliness; when a man lives the virtues, that is manliness.

Women and men strive for the same virtues, but often attain them and express them in different ways. The virtues will be lived and manifested differently in the lives of sisters, mothers, and wives than in brothers, husbands, and fathers. Two different musical instruments, playing the exact same notes, will produce two different sounds. The difference in the sounds is one of those ineffable things that is hard to describe with words, but easy to discern. Neither instrument is better than the other; in the hands of the diligent and dedicated, each instrument plays music that fills the spirit and adds beauty to the world.

A man's path to virtuous excellence begins with his pursuit of the seven manly virtues. These virtues, if diligently sought after and lived, will help a man unlock his fullest power and potential. The seven virtues are:

- Manliness
- Courage
- Industry
- Resolution
- Self-Reliance
- Discipline
- Honor

These seven virtues can be striven for by any man, in any situation. Rich or poor, young or old, married or single. From the soldier to the civilian, from the corporate warrior to the stay-at-home dad, the path of virtuous excellence is open to and vital for all men.

Why just seven and why these particular virtues? Shouldn't a man develop virtues like compassion and humility? Of course. Being a complete man means nurturing your tender side as well.

These seven virtues simply form the pole stars in the great constellation of manliness, providing men a sense of direction and leading them on the path to greatness. They are the virtues that have most called to the masculine spirit throughout the ages and which form the backbone of a man's pursuit of the virtuous life, a firm foundation upon which all the other virtues can be built.

We've organized the book into seven chapters, one for each of the seven manly virtues. Each chapter is filled with excerpts from books, speeches, letters, and poems that span the ages and are designed to help you better understand the virtues and inspire you to live them more fully.

We've included selections from the timeless works of ancient philosophers like Aristotle and Epictetus, virile speeches from Theodore Roosevelt and Winston Churchill, and manly poems from Rudyard Kipling and Henry Wadsworth Longfellow.

You'll also find excerpts from "success manuals" from the nineteenth and early twentieth centuries scattered throughout *Manvotionals*. Unlike much of the success and self-improvement literature pumped out today, which focuses primarily on positive thinking and superficial tips on becoming rich, muscular, and suave, success books from the turn of the twentieth century concentrated on developing a man's *character*. Our great-grandfathers believed that if a man worked sufficiently hard on forging a noble character, success in all the other areas of his life would naturally follow. Moreover, the idea of success that many of these books aspired to wasn't necessarily fame and fortune, but rather a life well lived filled with close relationships with family and friends, contentment with simple pleasures, and the peace of mind that comes from living a good, honest life.

For those reading literature from this genre and period for the first time, the earnest tone of the authors may seem a bit jarring. Living in a very cynical age, we're not used to such unabashed, guileless sincerity. But it will grow on you, trust us. Authors of this time had a knack for writing in a way that gets right to the heart of the matter and offers true insight.

Also, you'll probably notice that our selections come from the annals of Western thought. While we understand and appreciate that all cultures have inspiring views on manliness, we decided to focus on the Western tradition of masculinity for a couple of reasons. First, it narrowed our field of choices, providing us some much-needed focus and making the already incredibly difficult job of narrowing the vast field of potential entries a bit easier. And second, as the book will primarily be read by those living in Western countries, we thought it would be more interesting and engaging to explore the history and meaning of manliness within the culture in which readers have been immersed.

Finally, all the selections were chosen simply on the basis of readability, strength, and wisdom. The selections are long enough to impart profound insight and short enough to remain engaging. Too many anthologies like this one end up gathering dust on the coffee table. This book is not designed to make you feel good simply for purchasing it; it is not an ornamental piece for your bookshelf. It is designed to be read and pondered. Each selection was thoughtfully and carefully chosen to hit you right in the heart and inspire you to be a better man. We challenge you to read at least one selection every morning, allowing yourself to meditate upon it during the day. We promise that if you do this, you will grow as a man and will walk a little taller and be a little better by the time you turn the last page.

AUTHORS' NOTE: Selections have been edited for readability and length. The original spelling and punctuation of excerpts has been retained in most cases.

CHAPTER ONE
MANLINESS

Mention the word *manliness* these days and you'll probably be greeted with snorts and giggles. Many people today associate manliness with cartoonish images of men sitting in their "man caves," drinking beer and watching the big game. Or, just as likely, they don't think much about manliness at all, chalking it up to the mere possession of a certain set of anatomy. Whatever image they have in mind when you mention "manliness," it isn't usually positive, and it probably has nothing to do with virtue.

But if you search the annals of Western thought, you'll discover that this shallow conception of manliness is relatively new. For over two thousand years, many of the world's great thinkers explored and celebrated the subject of manliness, imagining it not as something silly or biologically inherent, but as the culmination of the virtues as expressed in the life of a man. Manliness was considered a virtue in and of itself, the attainment of which had to be actively pursued.

The epic poetry of the ancient Greeks praised the manliness of their heroes while their philosophy linked virtuous manhood to the health and longevity of society. Throughout the eighteenth century, great statesman tied the cultivation of true manliness to the success of emerging experiments in liberty and democracy. And into the early 1900s, writers encouraged men to embrace manliness as the crown of character and virtue.

This nearly two-thousand-year-old tradition of extolling manliness as a necessary and laudatory aspiration came to an end in the mid-twentieth century. Discussion of character and virtue fell out of favor in general, and talking about manliness as a specific virtue disappeared during our cultural experiment with gender neutrality. Praising manliness became verboten; disparaging it did not. And thus manliness became fodder for broad sitcoms and juvenile magazines.

We'd like to bring back the idea of manliness as a real, distinct virtue, a goal which all men should orient their lives toward. The following chapter highlights some of the best writings we've found on the topic of manliness itself. The selections, ranging from ancient Greek poetry to passages from nineteenth-century "success manuals," show that far from being the hazy concept it is seen as today, the definition of true manliness has been clear and consistent for thousands of years.

The selections are designed not only to explain what true, honorable manliness looks like and consists of, but also to resonate on a deeper level, giving you an idea of what manliness *feels* like. We hope that as you read this chapter, you will be inspired to place the ideal of manliness ever before you.

Wanted—A Man

FROM *PUSHING TO THE FRONT*, 1911
By Orison Swett Marden

Over the door of every profession, every occupation, every calling, the world has a standing advertisement: "Wanted—A Man."

Wanted, a man who will not lose his individuality in a crowd, a man who has the courage of his convictions, who is not afraid to say "No," though all the world say "Yes."

Wanted, a man who is larger than his calling, who considers it a low estimate of his occupation to value it merely as a means of getting a living. Wanted, a man who sees self-development, education and culture, discipline and drill, character and manhood, in his occupation.

Wanted, a man of courage who is not a coward in any part of his nature.

Wanted, a man who is symmetrical, and not one-sided in his development, who has not sent all the energies of his being into one narrow specialty and allowed all the other branches of his life to wither and die.

Wanted, a man who is broad, who does not take half views of things; a man who mixes common sense with his theories, who does not let a college education spoil him for practical, every-day life; a man who prefers substance to show, and one who regards his good name as a priceless treasure.

Wanted, a man "who, no stunted ascetic, is full of life and fire, but whose passions are trained to heed a strong will, the servant of a tender conscience; who has learned to love all beauty, whether of nature or of art, to hate all vileness, and to respect others as himself."

The world wants a man who is educated all over; whose nerves are brought to their acutest sensibility; whose brain is cultured, keen, incisive, broad; whose hands are deft; whose eyes are alert, sensitive, microscopic; whose heart is tender, magnanimous, true.

The whole world is looking for such a man. Although there are millions out of employment, yet it is almost impossible to find just the right man in almost any department of life, and yet everywhere we see the advertisement: "Wanted—A Man."

It is a sad sight to see thousands of students graduated every year from our grand institutions whose object is to make stalwart, independent, self-supporting men, turned out into the world saplings instead of stalwart oaks, "memory-glands" instead of brainy men, helpless instead of self-supporting, sickly instead of robust, weak instead of strong, leaning instead of erect. "So many promising youths, and never a finished man!"

The character sympathizes with and unconsciously takes on the nature of the body. A peevish, snarling, ailing man can not develop the vigor and strength of character which is possible to a healthy, robust, cheerful man. There is an inherent love in the human mind for *wholeness*, a demand that man shall come up to the highest standard; and there is an inherent protest or contempt for preventable deficiency. Nature, too, demands that man be ever at the top of his condition.

The first requisite of all education and discipline should be man-timber. Tough timber must come from well grown, sturdy trees. Such wood can be turned into a mast, can be fashioned into a piano or an exquisite carving. But it must become timber first. Time and patience develop the sapling into the tree. So through discipline, education, experience, the sapling child is developed into hardy mental, moral, physical man-timber.

If the youth should start out with the fixed determination that every statement he makes shall be the exact truth; that every promise he makes shall be redeemed to the letter; that every appointment shall be kept with the strictest faithfulness and with full regard for other men's time; if he should hold his reputation as a priceless treasure, feel that the eyes of the world are upon him, that he must not deviate a hair's breadth from the truth and right; if he should take such a stand at the outset, he would ... come to have almost unlimited credit and the confidence of everybody who knows him.

What are palaces and equipages; what though a man could cover a continent with his title-deeds, or an ocean with his commerce; compared with conscious rectitude, with a face that never turns pale at the accuser's voice, with a bosom that never throbs with fear of exposure, with a heart that might be turned inside out and disclose no stain of dishonor? To have done no man a wrong; ... to walk and live, unseduced, within arm's length of what is not your own, with nothing between your desire and its gratification but the invisible law of rectitude— *this is to be a man.*

> *"The superior man is he who develops, in harmonious proportions, his moral, intellectual, and physical nature. This should be the end at which men of all classes should aim, and it is this only which constitutes real greatness."* —Douglas Jerrold

A Manly Character

FROM *MEDITATIONS*, C. 170–180 A.D.
By Marcus Aurelius

In his *Meditations*, the Roman Emperor Marcus Aurelius (161–180 C.E.) sets out his personal ideas on Stoic philosophy. He begins his writings by describing what each of his mentors taught him about being a man.

From my grandfather Verus I learned good morals and the government of my temper.

From the reputation and remembrance of my father, modesty and a manly character.

From my mother, piety and beneficence, and abstinence, not only from evil deeds, but even from evil thoughts; and further, simplicity in my way of living, far removed from the habits of the rich.

From my great-grandfather, not to have frequented public schools, and to have had good teachers at home, and to know that on such things a man should spend liberally.

From my governor, to be neither of the green nor of the blue party at the games in the Circus, nor a partizan either of the Parmularius or the Scutarius at the gladiators' fights; from him too I learned endurance of labour, and to want little, and to work with my own hands, and not to meddle with other people's affairs, and not to be ready to listen to slander.

From Diognetus, not to busy myself about trifling things, and not to give credit to what was said by miracle-workers and jugglers about incantations and the driving away of daemons and such things; and not to breed quails for fighting, nor to give myself up passionately to such things; and to endure freedom of speech; and to have become intimate with philosophy; and to have been a hearer, first of Bacchius, then of Tandasis and Marcianus; and to have written dialogues in my youth; and to have desired a plank bed and skin, and whatever else of the kind belongs to the Grecian discipline.

From Rusticus I received the impression that my character required improvement and discipline; and from him I learned not to be led astray to sophistic emulation, nor to writing on speculative matters, nor to delivering little hortatory orations, nor to showing myself off as a man who practises much discipline, or does benevolent acts in order to make a display; … and not to walk about in the house in my outdoor dress, nor to do other things of the kind; and to write my letters with simplicity, like the letter which Rusticus wrote from Sinuessa to my mother; and with respect to those who have offended me by words, or done me wrong, to be easily disposed to be pacified and reconciled, as soon as they have shown a readiness to be reconciled; and to read carefully, and not to be satisfied with a superficial understanding of a book; nor hastily to give my assent to those who talk overmuch; and I am indebted to him for being acquainted with the discourses of Epictetus, which he communicated to me out of his own collection.

From Apollonius I learned freedom of will and undeviating steadiness of purpose; and to look to nothing else, not even for a moment, except to reason; ... and to see clearly in a living example that the same man can be both most resolute and yielding, and not peevish in giving his instruction; and to have had before my eyes a man who clearly considered his experience and his skill in expounding philosophical principles as the smallest of his merits; and from him I learned how to receive from friends what are esteemed favours, without being either humbled by them or letting them pass unnoticed.

From Sextus, a benevolent disposition, and the example of a family governed in a fatherly manner, and the idea of living conformably to nature; and gravity without affectation, and to look carefully after the interests of friends, and to tolerate ignorant persons, and those who form opinions without consideration: he had the power of readily accommodating himself to all, so that intercourse with him was more agreeable than any flattery; and at the same time he was most highly venerated by those who associated with him: and he had the faculty both of discovering and ordering, in an intelligent and methodical way, the principles necessary for life; and he never showed anger or any other passion, but was entirely free from passion, and also most affectionate; and he could express approbation without noisy display, and he possessed much knowledge without ostentation.

From Alexander the grammarian, to refrain from fault-finding, and not in a reproachful way to chide those who uttered any barbarous or solecistic or strange-sounding expression; but dexterously to introduce the very expression which ought to have been used, and in the way of answer or giving confirmation, or joining in an inquiry about the thing itself, not about the word, or by some other fit suggestion.

From Fronto I learned to observe what envy, and duplicity, and hypocrisy are in a tyrant, and that generally those among us who are called Patricians are rather deficient in paternal affection.

From Alexander the Platonic, not frequently nor without necessity to say to any one, or to write in a letter, that I have no leisure; nor continually to excuse the neglect of duties required by our relation to those with whom we live, by alleging urgent occupations.

From Catulus, not to be indifferent when a friend finds fault, even if he should find fault without reason, but to try to restore him to his usual disposition; and to be ready to speak well of teachers, as it is reported of Domitius and Athenodotus; and to love my children truly.

From my brother Severus, to love my kin, and to love truth, and to love justice; and through him I learned to know Thrasea, Helvidius, Cato, Dion, Brutus; and from him I received the idea of a polity in which there is the same law for all, a polity administered with regard to equal rights and equal freedom of speech, and the idea of a kingly government which respects most of all the freedom of the governed; I learned from him also consistency and undeviating steadiness in my regard for philosophy; and a disposition to do good, and to give to others readily, and to cherish good hopes, and to believe that I am loved by my friends; and in him I observed no concealment of his opinions with respect to those whom he condemned, and that his friends had no need to conjecture what he wished or did not wish, but it was quite plain.

From Maximus I learned self-government, and not to be led aside by anything; and cheerfulness in all circumstances, as well as in illness; and a just admixture in the moral character of sweetness and dignity, and to do what was set before me without complaining. I observed that everybody believed that he thought as he spoke, and that in all that he did he never had any bad intention; and he never showed amazement and surprise, and was never in a hurry, and never put off doing a thing, nor was perplexed nor dejected, nor did he ever laugh to disguise his vexation, nor, on the other hand, was he ever passionate or suspicious. He was accustomed to do acts of beneficence, and was ready to forgive, and was free from all falsehood; and he presented the appearance of a man who could not be diverted from right rather than of a man who had been improved. I observed, too, that no man could ever think that he was despised by Maximus, or ever venture to think himself a better man. He had also the art of being humorous in an agreeable way.

> *"I mean to make myself a man, and if I succeed in that, I shall succeed in everything else." —James A. Garfield*

Manhood

FROM *MEMORIES OF CHILDHOOD AND OTHER POEMS*, 1895
By John M. Morse

From the zenith afar, with its vertical ray—
Shines the sun in its splendor, the glory of day.
Tho' dark clouds should arise to bedim its clear light,
They are scattered away by its power and might.

In the noontide of life there is strength for the hour;
It is then that man reaches his zenith of power.
With an arm for the conflict, a brain that can plan—
All his trials but make him a *manlier man.*

Like the oak on the hillside, majestic in form:
Like the ship on the ocean, prepared for the storm;
When that storm would engulf, or would dash to the ground,
They come forth from the conflict with victory crowned.

What a power for good is a man in his prime,
Who will stand for the right with a firmness sublime;
Who will stand in his place with truth's banner unfurled,
Who will let his light shine for the good of the world.

When an enemy threatens the life of the State,
When all own, with sad hearts, that the peril is great;

When devouring flames shoot up higher and higher,
And destruction stalks forth as a fiend in the fire—

When by famine or sword, or by pestilence dread,
Many thousands are called to lie down with the dead.
When gross evils abound, and the wicked increase,
And we sigh for the joys and the triumphs of peace—

In such perilous times man's true manhood appears:
It has grown with his growth and has strengthened with years.
When his country needs help—when the danger is nigh—
He is ready, if need be, to dare and to die!

When the fiend in the fire has his victims at bay,
Or when famine and sword by the thousands would slay;
Or when pestilence—swift—for its victims would fly—
Then true manhood shines forth, brightest star in the sky.

"The greatest thing a man can possibly do in this world is to make the most possible out of the stuff that has been given him. This is success, and there is no other. It is not a question of what someone else can do or become which every youth should ask himself, but what can I do? How can I develop myself into the grandest possible manhood?" —Orison Swett Marden

Manliness in the Life of Jack London
FROM *THE BOOK OF JACK LONDON*
By Charmian London, 1921

Manliness involves living a life of *arete*, the excellence born from seeking to use up every last drop of one's potential and abilities.

Jack London led such a life. His supposed credo was:

"I would rather be ashes than dust!
I would rather that my spark should burn out in a brilliant blaze than it
   should be stifled by dry-rot.
I would rather be a superb meteor, every atom of me in magnificent glow,
   than a sleepy and permanent planet.
The function of man is to live, not to exist.
I shall not waste my days trying to prolong them.
I shall use my time."

And use his time he did. London saw the life of man as a struggle against the harshness of nature; a man had to ever be working to escape its unmerciful hand. To that end, London led a life of great hustle and adventure. Emerging from a childhood of poverty, he was a largely self-educated man willing to do everything and anything to get ahead and make the most of life. He labored 12–18 hours a day in a mill, laundry, and cannery, shoveled coal at a power station, bought his own sloop and took to the seas as a sailor and oyster pirate, spent time as a hobo, and sought for riches as a prospector in the rugged Alaskan wilderness. When he began to pursue his true dream—making a living as a writer—he faced one rejection after another.

But London prevailed, writing over fifty books (*The Call of the Wild* being his most famous) and hundreds of short stories, serving as a wartime correspondent, and becoming the highest paid writer of his time. Success allowed him to pursue other endeavors—ranching and farming, horseback riding, sailing, and traveling to name a few. His was a life not without faults or struggles, but when London died at age 40 from uremia, he had accomplished and experienced more in those few decades than many men do when given twice as much time.

In this first selection, W. B. Hargrave, who spent time with Jack London during the Klondike Gold Rush, recalls his impressions of the man. A portrait of London as sharp in mind, rugged in spirit, and zealous for life, it offers a rich snapshot of manliness.

It was in October of 1897 that I first met him ... No other man has left so indelible an impression upon my memory as Jack London. He was but a boy then, in years ... But he possessed the mental equipment of a mature man, and I have never thought of him as a boy except in the heart of him ... the clean, joyous, tender, unembittered heart of youth. His personality would challenge attention anywhere. Not only in his beauty for he was a handsome lad but there was about him that indefinable something that distinguishes genius from mediocrity. Though a youth, he displayed none of the insolent egotism of youth; he was *an idealist who went after the attainable;* a dreamer who was a man among strong men; a man who faced life with superb assurance and who could face death serenely imperturbable. These were my first impressions; which months of companionship only confirmed.

He was one of the few adventurers, of the thousands whom the lure of gold enticed to the frozen fastnesses of the Klondike, whose hardihood and pluck scaled the summit of Chilkoot Pass that year. His cabin was on the bank of the Yukon, near the mouth of the Stewart River. I remember well the first time I entered it. London was seated on the edge of a bunk, rolling a cigarette. He smoked incessantly and it would have taken no Sherlock Holmes to tell what the stains on his fingers meant. One of his partners, Goodman, was preparing a meal, and the other, Sloper, was doing some carpentry work. From the few words which I overheard as I entered, I surmised that Jack had challenged some of Goodman's orthodox views, and that the latter was doggedly defending himself in an unequal contest of wits. Many times afterward I myself felt the rapier thrust of London's, and knew how to sympathize with Goodman.

Jack interrupted the conversation to welcome me, and his hospitality was so cordial, his smile so genial, his goodfellowship so real, that it instantly dispelled all reserve. I was invited to participate in the discussion, which I did, much to my subsequent discomfiture.

That day—the day on which our friendship began—has become consecrated in my memory. I find it difficult to write about Jack without laying myself open to the charge of adulation. During the course of my life ... I have met men who were worth while; but Jack was the one man with whom I have come in personal contact who possessed the qualities of heart and mind that made him one of the world's overshadowing geniuses.

He was intrinsically kind and *irrationally generous* .... With an innate refinement, a gentleness that had survived the roughest of associations. Sometimes he would become silent and reflective, but he was never morose or sullen. His silence was an attentive silence. I have known him to end a discussion by merely assuming the attitude of a courteous listener, and when his indiscreet opponent had tangled himself in the web of his own illogic, and had perhaps fallen back upon invective to bolster his position, Jack would calmly roll another cigarette, and throwing his head back, give vent to infectious laughter—infectious because it was never bitter or derisive .... He was always good-natured; he was more—he was charmingly cheerful. If in those days he was beset by melancholia, he concealed it from his companions.

Inasmuch as Louis Savard's cabin was the largest and most comfortable it became the popular meeting place for the denizens of the camp. Louis had constructed a large fireplace, and my recollections of London are intertwined with the many hours we spent together in front of its cheerful light. Many a long night he and I, outlasting the vigil of the others, sat before the blazing spruce logs, and talked the hours away. A brave figure of a man he was, lounging by the crude fireplace, its light playing on his handsome features—a face that one would look at twice even in the crowded city street. In appearance older than his years; a body lithe and strong; neck bared at the throat; a tangled cluster of brown hair that fell low over his brow and which he was wont to brush back impatiently when engaged in animated conversation; a sensitive mouth, but lips, nevertheless, that could set in serious and masterful lines; a radiant smile, marred by two missing teeth (lost, he told me, in a fight on shipboard); eyes that often carried an introspective expression; the face of an artist and a dreamer, but with strong lines denoting will power and boundless energy. An outdoor man—in short, a real man, a man's man.

He had a mental craving for the truth. He applied one test to religion, to economics, to everything. "What is the truth?" "What is just?" It was with these questions that he confronted the baffling enigma of life. He could think great thoughts. One could not meet him without feeling the impact of a superior intellect.

Many and diverse were the subjects we discussed, often with the silent Louis as our only listener. Our views did not always coincide, and on one occasion when argument had waxed long and hot and London had finally left us, with only the memory of his glorious smile to salve my defeat, Louis looked up from his game of solitaire (which I think he played because it required no conversation) and became veritably verbose. This is what he said: "You mak' ver' good talk, but zat London he too damn smart for you."

Jack London on Man's Infinite Potential
EXCERPT FROM *THE IRON HEEL*
By Jack London, 1908

The second selection pertaining to Jack London's idea of manliness comes from London's fictional novel, *The Iron Heel*, published in 1908. The narrator,

Avis Everhard, describes her husband and shares his favorite poem, one which speaks to the infinite power and potential of man and the desire to live life to the fullest:

· ·

But he had pride. How could he have been an eagle and not have pride? His contention was that it was finer for a finite mortal speck of life to feel Godlike, than for a god to feel godlike; and so it was that he exalted what he deemed his mortality. He was fond of quoting a fragment from a certain poem. He had never seen the whole poem, and he had tried vainly to learn its authorship. I here give the fragment, not alone because he loved it, but because it epitomized the paradox that he was in the spirit of him, and his conception of his spirit. For how can a man, with thrilling, and burning, and exaltation, recite the following and still be mere mortal earth, a bit of fugitive force, an evanescent form? Here it is:

"Joy upon joy and gain upon gain
Are the destined rights of my birth,
And I shout the praise of my endless days
To the echoing edge of the earth.
Though I suffer all deaths that a man can die
To the uttermost end of time,
I have deep-drained this, my cup of bliss,
In every age and clime—

The froth of Pride, the tang of Power,
The sweet of Womanhood!
I drain the lees upon my knees,
For oh, the draught is good;
I drink to Life, I drink to Death,
And smack my lips with song,
For when I die, another 'I' shall pass the cup along.

The man you drove from Eden's grove
Was I, my Lord, was I,
And I shall be there when the earth and the air
Are rent from sea to sky;
For it is my world, my gorgeous world,
The world of my dearest woes,
From the first faint cry of the newborn
To the rack of the woman's throes.

Packed with the pulse of an unborn race,
Torn with a world's desire,
The surging flood of my wild young blood
Would quench the judgment fire.
I am Man, Man, Man, from the tingling flesh
To the dust of my earthly goal,
From the nestling gloom of the pregnant womb
To the sheen of my naked soul.

Bone of my bone and flesh of my flesh
The whole world leaps to my will,
And the unslaked thirst of an Eden cursed
Shall harrow the earth for its fill.
Almighty God, when I drain life's glass
Of all its rainbow gleams,
The hapless plight of eternal night
Shall be none too long for my dreams.

The man you drove from Eden's grove
Was I, my Lord, was I,
And I shall be there when the earth and the air
Are rent from sea to sky;
For it is my world, my gorgeous world,
The world of my dear delight,

From the brightest gleam of the Arctic stream
To the dusk of my own love-night."

"One cannot always be a hero, but one can always be a man." —Johann Wolfgang von Goethe

The Song of the Manly Men

FROM *THE SONG OF THE MANLY MEN AND OTHER VERSES*, 1908
By Frank Hudson

Heard from the wild and the desert,
Echoing back from the sea,
Faint o'er the din of the city
Floats the song of the men that are free.
There's a lilt in the strenuous chorus,
There's joy in our labouring when
We hear o'er the babble of weaklings
The song of the manly men.

'Tis heard 'mid the ringing of anvils,
'Tis heard 'mid the clashing of steel,
When the hosts go down together,
And the shell-slashed legions reel.
'Tis heard from the mine and the furrow;
From prairie, and mountain, and glen;
Like the roll of the drums in the distance
Comes the song of the manly men.

The fool in his ignorant bondage
May sneer at their fashion and speech,
The fop and the feather-bed workman

Make mock of the lesson they teach.

The demagogues rant in the market

Of things high removed from their ken:

What are words—empty words—in the balance

With the deeds of the manly men?

They are vertebrate, keen, and courageous,

These toilers, who raise the refrain;

Their work swept away by disaster—

Undaunted, they build it again.

Yet ye fawn on your quacks and your idols,

Your dreamers and mountebanks—then,

When your country is suffering shipwreck,

You'll fall back on the manly men.

The American Boy

FROM *THE STRENUOUS LIFE: ESSAYS AND ADDRESSES*, 1900
By Theodore Roosevelt

Of course what we have a right to expect of the American boy is that he shall turn out to be a good American man. Now, the chances are strong that he won't be much of a man unless he is a good deal of a boy. He must not be a coward or a weakling, a bully, a shirk, or a prig. He must work hard and play hard. He must be clean-minded and clean-lived, and able to hold his own under all circumstances and against all comers. It is only on these conditions that he will grow into the kind of American man of whom America can be really proud.

The boy can best become a good man by being a good boy—not a goody-goody boy, but just a plain good boy. I do not mean that he must love only the negative virtues; I mean he must love the positive virtues also. "Good," in the largest sense, should include whatever is fine, straightforward, clean, brave, and manly. The best boys I know—the best men I know—are good at their studies or their business, fearless and stalwart, hated and feared by all that is wicked and depraved, incapable of submitting to wrong-doing, and equally incapable of being aught but tender to the weak and helpless. A healthy-minded boy should feel hearty contempt for the coward, and even more hearty indignation for the boy who bullies girls or small boys, or tortures animals. One prime reason for abhorring cowards is because every good boy should have it in him to thrash the objectionable boy as the need arises.

Of course the effect that a thoroughly manly, thoroughly straight and upright boy can have upon the companions of his own age, and upon those who are younger, is incalculable. If he is not thoroughly manly, then they will not respect him, and his good qualities will count for but little; while, of course, if he is mean, cruel, or wicked, then his physical strength and force of mind merely make him so much the more objectionable a member of society. He cannot do good work if he is not strong and does not try with his whole heart and soul to count in any contest; and his strength will be a curse to himself and to every one else if he does not have thorough command over himself and over his own evil passions, and if he does not use his strength on the side of decency, justice, and fair dealing.

In short, in life, as in a football game, the principle to follow is: Hit the line hard; don't foul and don't shirk, but hit the line hard!

"A man must stand erect, not be kept erect by others."
—*Marcus Aurelius*

Character of the Happy Warrior

FROM *POEMS, IN TWO VOLUMES*, 1807
By William Wordsworth

Who is the happy Warrior? Who is he
That every Man in arms should wish to be?
—It is the generous Spirit, who, when brought
Among the tasks of real life, hath wrought
Upon the plan that pleased his childish thought:
Whose high endeavours are an inward light
That makes the path before him always bright:
Who, with a natural instinct to discern
What knowledge can perform, is diligent to learn;
Abides by this resolve, and stops not there,
But makes his moral being his prime care;
Who, doomed to go in company with Pain,
And Fear, and Bloodshed, miserable train!
Turns his necessity to glorious gain;
In face of these doth exercise a power
Which is our human nature's highest dower;
Controls them and subdues, transmutes, bereaves
Of their bad influence, and their good receives;
By objects, which might force the soul to abate
Her feeling, rendered more compassionate;
Is placable—because occasions rise
So often that demand such sacrifice;
More skilful in self-knowledge, even more pure,
As tempted more; more able to endure,
As more exposed to suffering and distress;
Thence, also, more alive to tenderness.
—'Tis he whose law is reason; who depends
Upon that law as on the best of friends;

Whence, in a state where men are tempted still
To evil for a guard against worse ill,
And what in quality or act is best
Doth seldom on a right foundation rest,
He fixes good on good alone, and owes
To virtue every triumph that he knows:
—Who, if he rise to station of command,
Rises by open means; and there will stand
On honourable terms, or else retire,
And in himself possess his own desire;
Who comprehends his trust, and to the same
Keeps faithful with a singleness of aim;
And therefore does not stoop, nor lie in wait
For wealth, or honours, or for worldly state;
Whom they must follow; on whose head must fall,
Like showers of manna, if they come at all:
Whose powers shed round him in the common strife,
Or mild concerns of ordinary life,
A constant influence, a peculiar grace;
But who, if he be called upon to face
Some awful moment to which heaven has joined
Great issues, good or bad for human kind,
Is happy as a Lover; and attired
With sudden brightness, like a Man inspired;
And, through the heat of conflict, keeps the law
In calmness made, and sees what he foresaw;
Or if an unexpected call succeed,
Come when it will, is equal to the need:
—He who, though thus endued as with a sense
And faculty for storm and turbulence,
Is yet a Soul whose master-bias leans

To homefelt pleasures and to gentle scenes;
Sweet images! which, wheresoe'er he be,
Are at his heart; and such fidelity
It is his darling passion to approve;
More brave for this, that he hath much to love:—
'Tis, finally, the Man, who, lifted high,
Conspicuous object in a Nation's eye,
Or left unthought-of in obscurity,
Who, with a toward or untoward lot,
Prosperous or adverse, to his wish or not,
Plays, in the many games of life, that one
Where what he most doth value must be won:
Whom neither shape of danger can dismay,
Nor thought of tender happiness betray;
Who, not content that former worth stand fast,
Looks forward, persevering to the last,
From well to better, daily self-surpast:
Who, whether praise of him must walk
    the earth
For ever, and to noble deeds give birth,
Or He must go to dust without his fame,
And leave a dead unprofitable name,
Finds comfort in himself and in
    his cause;
And, while the mortal mist is
    gathering, draws
His breath in confidence of
    Heaven's applause:
This is the happy Warrior; this is He
Whom every Man in arms should
    wish to be.

MANLINESS

> *"It is very sad for a man to make himself servant to a single thing; his manhood all taken out of him by the hydraulic pressure of excessive business. I should not like to be merely a doctor, a great lawyer, a great minister, a great politician. I should like to be, also, something of a man."* —Theodore Parker

A Truly Great Man

FROM "THE BUSY-BODY, NO. III," 1728
By Benjamin Franklin

It is said, that the Persians, in their ancient constitution, had public schools, in which virtue was taught as a liberal art or science: and it is certainly of more consequence to a man, that he has learnt to govern his passions, in spite of temptation; to be just in his dealings, to be temperate in his

pleasures, to support himself with fortitude under his misfortunes, to behave with prudence, in all his affairs, and in every circumstance of life; I say, it is of much more real advantage to him to be thus qualified, than to be a master of all the arts and sciences in the world beside.

Almost every man has a strong natural desire of being valued and esteemed by the rest of his species; but I am concerned and grieved to see how few fall into the right and only infallible method of becoming so. That laudable ambition is too commonly misapplied, and often ill employed. Some, to make themselves considerable, pursue learning; others grasp at wealth; some aim at being thought witty; and others are only careful to make the most of an handsome person: but what is wit, or wealth, or form, or learning, when compared with virtue? It is true, we love the handsome, we applaud the learned, and we fear the rich and powerful; but we even worship and adore the virtuous. Nor is it strange; since men of virtue are so rare, so very rare to be found. If we were as industrious to become good, as to make ourselves great, we should become really great by being good, and the number of valuable men be much increased; but it is a grand mistake to think of being great without goodness; and I pronounce it as certain, that there never was yet a truly great man, that was not at the same time truly virtuous.

"We need the iron qualities that go with true manhood. We need the positive virtues of resolution, of courage, of indomitable will, of power to do without shrinking the rough work that must always be done." —Theodore Roosevelt

The Man From the Crowd
FROM *SONGS OF THE AVERAGE MAN*, 1907
By Sam Walter Foss

Men seem as alike as the leaves on the trees,
As alike as the bees in a swarming of bees;
And we look at the millions that make up the state
All equally little and equally great,
And the pride of our courage is cowed.
Then Fate calls for a man who is larger than men—
There's a surge in the crowd—there's a movement—and then

There arises a man that is larger than men—
And the man comes up from the crowd.

The chasers of trifles run hither and yon,
And the little small days of small things still go on,
And the world seems no better at sunset than dawn,
And the race still increases its plentiful spawn.
And the voice of our wailing is loud.
Then the Great Deed calls out for the Great Man to come,
And the crowd, unbelieving, sits sullen and dumb—
But the Great Deed is done, for the Great Man is come—
Aye, the man comes up from the crowd.

There's a dead hum of voices, all say the same thing,
And our forefathers' songs are the songs that we sing,
And the deeds by our fathers and grandfathers done
Are done by the son of the son of the son,
And our heads in contrition are bowed.
Lo, a call for a man who shall make all things new
Goes down through the throng! See! He rises in view!
Make room for the men who shall make all things new!—
For the man who comes up from the crowd.

And where is the man who comes up from the throng

Who does the new deed and who sings the new song,

And makes the old world as a world that is new?

And who is the man? It is you! It is you!

And our praise is exultant and proud.

We are waiting for you there—for you are the man!

Come up from the jostle as soon as you can;

Come up from the crowd there, for you are the man—

The man who comes up from the crowd.

> *"Life is too short to be little. Man is never so manly as when he feels deeply, acts boldly, and expresses himself with frankness and with fervor." —Benjamin Disraeli*

True Manliness
FROM *EVERY-DAY RELIGION*, 1886
By James Freeman Clarke

Manliness means perfect manhood, as womanliness implies perfect womanhood. Manliness is the character of a man as he ought to be, as he was meant to be. It expresses the qualities which go to make a perfect man— truth, courage, conscience, freedom, energy, self-possession, self-control. But it does not exclude gentleness, tenderness, compassion, modesty. A man is not less manly, but more so, because he is gentle. In fact, our word "gentleman" shows that a typical man must also be a gentle man.

By manly qualities the world is carried forward. The manly spirit shows itself in enterprise, the love of meeting difficulties and overcoming them—the resolution which will not yield, which patiently perseveres, and does not admit the possibility of defeat. It enjoys hard toil, rejoices in stern labor, is ready to make sacrifices, to suffer and bear disaster patiently. It is generous, giving itself to a good cause not its own; it is public-spirited, devoting itself to the general good with no expectation of reward. It is ready to defend unpopular truth, to stand by those who are wronged, to uphold the weak. Having resolved, it does not go back, but holds on, through good report and evil, sure that the right must win at last. And so it causes truth to prevail, and keeps up the standard of a noble purpose in the world.

In a recent awful disaster, amid the blackness and darkness and tempest, the implacable sea and the pitiless storm—when men's hearts were failing them from terror, and women and children had no support but faith in a Divine Providence and a coming immortality—the dreadful scene was illuminated by the courage and manly devotion of those who risked their own lives to save the lives of others. Such heroism is like a sunbeam breaking through the tempest. It shows us the real worth there is in man.

No matter how selfish mankind may seem, whenever hours like these come, which try men's souls, they show that the age of chivalry has not gone; that though, "The knights are dust, and their good swords rust," there are as high-hearted heroes now as ever. Firemen rush into a flaming house to save women and children. Sailors take their lives in their hands to rescue their fellow-men from a wreck. They save them at this great risk, not because they are friends or relatives, but because they are fellow-men.

Courage is an element of manliness. It is more than readiness to encounter danger and death, for we are not often called to meet such perils. It is every-day courage which is most needed—that which shrinks from no duty because it is difficult; which makes one ready to say what he believes, when his opinions are unpopular; which does not allow him to postpone a duty, but makes him ready to encounter it at once; a courage which is not afraid of ridicule when one believes himself right; which is not the slave of custom, the fool of fashion. … It does not seek display, it is often the courage of silence no less than speech; it is modest courage, unpretending though resolute. It holds fast to its convictions and principles, whether men hear or whether they forbear.

Truthfulness is another element of true manliness. Lies usually come from cowardice, because men are afraid of standing by their flag, because they shrink from opposition, or because they are conscious of something wrong which they cannot defend, and so conceal. Secret faults, secret purposes, habits of conduct of which we are ashamed, lead to falsehood, and falsehood is cowardice. … Therefore if we wish to be manly, we must not do anything of which we are ashamed. He who lives by firm principles of truth and right, who deceives no one, injures no one, who therefore has nothing to hide, he alone is manly. The bad man may be audacious, but he has no true courage. His manliness is only a pretense, an empty shell, a bold demeanor, with no real firmness behind it.

True manliness differs also from the false in its attitude to woman. Its knightly feeling makes it wish to defend her rights, to maintain her claims, to be her protector and advocate. False manliness wishes to show its superiority by treating women as inferiors. It flatters them, but it does not respect them. It fears their competition on equal levels, and wishes to keep them confined, not within walls … but behind the more subtle barriers of opinion, prejudice, and supposed feminine aptitudes. True manliness holds out the hand to woman, and says, "Do whatever you are able to do; whatever God meant you to do. Neither you nor I can tell what that is till all artificial barriers are removed, and you have full opportunity to try."

Manly strength respects womanly purity, sympathy, and grace of heart. And this is the real chivalry of the present hour.

"Masculinity is not something given to you, but something you gain. And you gain it by winning small battles with honor."
—*Norman Mailer*

Manliness Is Teachable

FROM *THE SUPPLIANT WOMEN*, 423 B.C.
By Euripides (translated by Frank William Jones)

In a battle outside the gates of Thebes, seven great Argive warriors are killed, but the ruler who takes power in that city, Creon, decrees that their bodies will be left to rot.

The mothers of the dead soldiers beg Athens to help them bring back the bodies of their dead sons so that they can be buried. The King of Athens has mercy on the mothers, attacks Thebes, and retrieves the corpses. The men are given a proper funeral.

In this selection from the poem, *The Suppliant Women*, Adrastus, the King of Argos, eulogizes the deeds and character of five of the dead soldiers. Each man who died was not only a great warrior, but embodied the characteristics of true manliness.

Hear, then. By granting me the privilege
Of praising friends, you meet my own desire
To speak of them with justice and with truth.
I saw the deeds—bolder than words can tell—
By which they hoped to take the city. Look:

The handsome one is Capaneus. Through him
The lightning went. A man of means, he never
Flaunted his wealth but kept an attitude
No prouder than a poor man's. He avoided
People who live beyond their needs and load
Their tables to excess. He used to say
That good does not consist in belly-food,
And satisfaction comes from moderation.
He was true in friendship to present and absent friends;
Not many men are so. His character
Was never false; his ways were courteous;
His word, in house or city, was his bond.

Second I name Eteoclus. He practiced
Another kind of virtue. Lacking means,
This youth held many offices in Argos.
Often his friends would make him gifts of gold,
But he never took them into his house. He wanted

No slavish way of life, haltered by money.
He kept his hate for sinners, not the city;
A town is not to blame if a bad pilot
Makes men speak ill of it.

Hippomedon, third of the heroes, showed his nature thus:
While yet a boy he had the strength of will
Not to take up the pleasures of the Muses
That soften life; he went to live in the country,
Giving himself hard tasks to do, rejoicing
In manly growth. He hunted, delighted in horses,
And stretched the bow with his hands, to make his body
Useful to the city.

There lies the son
Of huntress Atalanta, Parthenopaeus,
Supreme in beauty. He was Arcadian,
But came to Inachus' banks and was reared in Argos.
After his upbringing there, he showed himself,
As resident foreigners should, not troublesome
Or spiteful to the city, or disputatious,
Which would have made him hard to tolerate
As citizen and guest. He joined the army
Like a born Argive, fought the country's wars,
Was glad when the city prospered, took it hard
If bad times came. Although he had many lovers,
And women flocked to him, still he was careful
To cause them no offense.

In praise of Tydeus
I shall say much in little. He was ambitious,
Greatly gifted, and wise in deeds, not words.

From what I have told you, Theseus, you should not wonder

That these men dared to die before the towers.

To be well brought up develops self-respect:

Anyone who has practiced what is good

Is ashamed to turn out badly. Manliness

Is teachable. Even a child is taught

To say and hear what he does not understand;

Things understood are kept in mind till age.

So, in like manner, train your children well.

"Have an ambition to be remembered, not as a great lawyer, doctor, merchant, scientist, manufacturer, or scholar, but as a great man, every inch a king." —Charles Sumner

If—
By Rudyard Kipling, 1895

If you can keep your head when all about you

Are losing theirs and blaming it on you;

If you can trust yourself when all men doubt you,

But make allowance for their doubting too;

If you can wait and not be tired by waiting,

Or, being lied about, don't deal in lies,

Or, being hated, don't give way to hating,

And yet don't look too good, nor talk too wise:

If you can dream—and not make dreams your master;

If you can think—and not make thoughts your aim;

If you can meet with Triumph and Disaster

And treat those two impostors just the same;

If you can bear to hear the truth you've spoken

Twisted by knaves to make a trap for fools,
Or watch the things you gave your life to, broken,
And stoop and build 'em up with worn-out tools:

If you can make one heap of all your winnings
And risk it all on one turn of pitch-and-toss,
And lose, and start again at your beginnings
And never breathe a word about your loss;
If you can force your heart and nerve and sinew
To serve your turn long after they are gone,
And so hold on when there is nothing in you
Except the Will which says to them: "Hold on!"

If you can talk with crowds and keep your virtue,
Or walk with kings—nor lose the common touch;
If neither foes nor loving friends can hurt you;
If all men count with you, but none too much;
If you can fill the unforgiving minute
With sixty seconds' worth of distance run,
Yours is the Earth and everything that's in it,
And—which is more—you'll be a Man, my son!

CHAPTER TWO

COURAGE

Philosophers have attempted to define courage for millennia. Aristotle, in his *Nicomachean Ethics*, establishes perhaps the best working definition of this virtue. Courage, according to Aristotle, is the mean between fear and recklessness. Cowards shrink even from things that shouldn't be feared, while reckless men, buoyed by unwarranted confidence, take unnecessary risks. The courageous man, however, strikes a balance between irrational fear and fool-hardy recklessness. He fears that which should be feared but remains steadfast for the right reason. That right reason, according to Aristotle, is for the sake of honor and nobility. In short, courage consists of acknowledging rational fears but acting nobly despite these fears in order to maintain manly honor.

A man can display courage in different ways. Physical courage is the type of courage that often first comes to mind when we think about this virtue. Tales of brave soldiers charging up a hill amid whizzing bullets consume our boyish imaginations. We are inspired and humbled by the stories of firemen and police officers rushing into the burning towers on 9/11 while everyone else was running out. We all hope that when called upon in a crisis, we too would be willing to risk our physical safety to save the lives of others.

A man can also display intellectual courage. History is filled with great figures—men like Socrates, Descartes, Bacon, and Darwin—who faced persecution for their ideas, yet endured social sanction with manly courage. Because of their courage to think differently and stand up for their ideas, society advanced and improved.

Finally, a man can show moral courage. Moral courage can be defined as the determination to follow what one believes to be right, regardless of the cost to one's self, and irrespective of the disapproval of others. Moral courage has been displayed by great leaders like Gandhi and Martin Luther King Jr., and ordinary people like the Chinese protester who stood in the way of the tanks at Tiananmen Square, young American civil rights activists who faced down angry mobs, brutal fire hoses and ferocious dogs, and the saints and believers of many religions who chose punishment and death rather than the renunciation of their faith.

In this chapter, we've pulled together writings that discuss the many different expressions of courage. They demonstrate the way in which all three types—physical, intellectual, and moral—are vital not only in life's great challenges, but in the small day-to-day decisions we must make. Courage is needed not only in extreme acts of heroism but in the decision to uphold our more mundane commitments and promises. Courage grants us the strength not only to withstand danger but to approach life as a pioneer and adventurer, embracing risk and plunging ever forward into the unknown.

"Courage is rightly esteemed the first of human qualities because it is the quality which guarantees all others." —Winston Churchill

Courage Is the Standing Army of the Soul
FROM *MANHOOD, FAITH AND COURAGE*, 1906
By Henry Van Dyke

This is a sermon about courage—one of the simplest and most straightforward of the virtues; necessary, and therefore possible, for every true and noble human life.

It is a quality that we admire by instinct. We need no teacher to tell us that it is a fine thing to be brave. The lack of courage is universally recognized as a grave defect in character. If in our own hearts we feel the want of it, if we cannot find enough of it to enable us to face the dangers and meet the responsibilities and fight the battles of life, we are not only sorry, but secretly ashamed. The absence of courage is a fault that few are willing to confess. We naturally conceal it, and cover it up, and try to keep it secret even from ourselves. We invent favourable names for it, which are only unconscious excuses. We call it prudence, or respectability, or conservatism, or economy, or worldly wisdom, or the instinct of self-preservation. For in truth there is nothing that we are more reluctant to admit than cowardice; and there is no virtue which we would more gladly possess and prove than courage.

In the first place, it is an honourable virtue. Men have always loved and praised it. It lends a glory and a splendour to the life in which it dwells—lifts it up and ennobles it, and crowns it with light. The world delights in heroism, even in its rudest forms and lowest manifestations. Among the animals we create a sort of aristocracy on the basis of courage, and recognize, in the fearlessness of the game beasts and birds and fishes, a claim to rank above the timorous, furtive, spiritless members of creation.

And in man bravery is always fine. We salute it in our enemies. A daring foe is respected, and though we must fight against him we can still honour his courage, and almost forget the conflict in our admiration for his noble bearing. That is what Dr. Johnson meant by saying, "I love a good hater." The enemy who slinks and plots and conceals—makes traps and ambuscades, seeks to lead his opponent into dangers which he himself would never dare to face—is despicable, serpentine, and contemptible. But he who stands up boldly against his antagonist in any conflict, physical, social, or spiritual, and deals fair blows, and uses honest arguments, and faces the issues of warfare, is a man to love even across the chasm of strife … A brave, frank, manly foe is infinitely better than a false, weak, timorous friend.

In the second place, courage is a serviceable virtue. There is hardly any place in which it is not useful. There is no type of character, no sphere of action, in which there is not room and need for it.

Genius is talent set on fire by courage. Fidelity is simply daring to be true in small things as well as great. As many as are the conflicts and perils and hardships of life, so many are the uses and the forms of courage. It is necessary, indeed, as the protector and defender of all the other virtues. Courage is the standing army of the soul which keeps it from conquest, pillage, and slavery.

Unless we are brave we can hardly be truthful, or generous, or just, or pure, or kind, or loyal. "Few persons," says a wise observer, "have the courage to appear as good as they really are." You must be brave in order to fulfill your own possibilities of virtue. Courage is essential to guard the best qualities of the soul, and to clear the way for their action, and make them move with freedom and vigour.

If we desire to be good, we must first of all desire to be brave, that against all opposition, scorn, and danger we may move straight onward to do the right.

In the third place, courage is a comfortable virtue. It fills the soul with inward peace and strength; in fact this is just what it is—courage is simply strength of heart. Subjection to fear is weakness, bondage, feverish unrest. To be afraid is to have no soul that we can call our own; it is to be at the beck and call of alien powers, to be chained and driven and tormented; it is to lose the life itself in the anxious care to keep it. Many people are so afraid to die that they have never begun to live. But courage emancipates us and gives us to ourselves, that we may give ourselves freely and without fear to God. How sweet and clear and steady is the life into which this virtue enters day by day, not merely in those great flashes of excitement which come in the moments of crisis, but in the presence of the hourly perils, the continual conflicts. Not to tremble at the shadows which surround us, not to shrink from the foes who threaten us, not to hesitate and falter

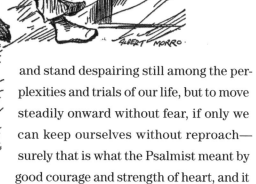

and stand despairing still among the perplexities and trials of our life, but to move steadily onward without fear, if only we can keep ourselves without reproach—surely that is what the Psalmist meant by good courage and strength of heart, and it is a most comfortable, pleasant, peaceful, and happy virtue.

There is a sharp distinction between courage and recklessness. The reckless man is ignorant; he rushes into danger without hesitation, simply because he does not know what danger means. The brave man is intelligent; he faces danger because he understands it and is prepared to meet it. The drunkard who runs, in the delirium of intoxication, into a burning house is not brave; he is only stupid. But the clear-eyed hero who makes his way, with every sense alert and every nerve strung, into the hell of flames to rescue some little child, proves his courage.

Courage does not consist in the absence of fear, but in the conquest of it. Timidity is no more inconsistent with courage than doubt is inconsistent with faith. For as faith is simply the overriding and subjugating of doubt by believing where you cannot prove, so courage is simply the conquest and suppression of fear by going straight on in the path of duty and love.

There is one more distinction that needs to be drawn—the distinction between courage and daring. This distinction is not in kind, but in degree. For daring is only a rare and exceptional kind of courage. It is for great occasions; the battle, the shipwreck, the conflagration. It is an inspiration; Emerson calls it "a flash of moral genius." But courage in the broader sense is an every-day virtue. It includes the possibility of daring, if it be called for; but from hour to hour, in the long, steady run of life, courage manifests itself in quieter, humbler forms—in patience under little trials, in perseverance in distasteful labours, in endurance of suffering, in resistance of continual and familiar temptations, in hope and cheerfulness and activity and fidelity and truthfulness and kindness, and such sweet, homely virtues as may find a place in the narrowest and most uneventful life.

There is no duty so small, no trial so slight, that it does not afford room for courage. It has a meaning and value for every phase of existence; for the workshop and for the battlefield, for the thronged city and for the lonely desert, for the sick-room and for the market-place, for the study and for the counting-house, for the church and for the drawing-room. There is courage physical, and social, and moral, and intellectual—a soldier's courage, a doctor's courage, a lawyer's courage, a preacher's courage, a nurse's courage, a merchant's courage, a man's courage, a woman's courage—for courage is just strength of heart, and the strong heart makes itself felt everywhere, and lifts up the whole of life, and ennobles it, and makes it move directly to its chosen aim.

"When a resolute young fellow steps up to the great bully, the World, and takes him boldly by the beard, he is often surprised to find it come off in his hand, and that it was only tied on to scare away timid adventurers." —Oliver Wendell Holmes

George Gray
FROM *SPOON RIVER ANTHOLOGY*, 1915
By Edgar Lee Masters

I have studied many times
The marble which was chiseled for me—

A boat with a furled sail at rest in a harbor.

In truth it pictures not my destination

But my life.

For love was offered me and I shrank from its disillusionment;

Sorrow knocked at my door, but I was afraid;

Ambition called to me, but I dreaded the chances.

Yet all the while I hungered for meaning in my life.

And now I know that we must lift the sail

And catch the winds of destiny

Wherever they drive the boat.

To put meaning in one's life may end in madness,

But life without meaning is the torture

Of restlessness and vague desire—

It is a boat longing for the sea and yet afraid.

"Courage charms us, because it indicates that a man loves an idea better than all things in the world, that he is thinking neither of his bed, nor his dinner, nor his money, but will venture all to put in act the invisible thought of his mind."
—Ralph Waldo Emerson

The Character of True Courage
FROM *NICOMACHEAN ETHICS*, C. 350 B.C.
By Aristotle

The same evils which terrify one person are not formidable to another; though there are some of such an irresistible nature, as to shake the firmest minds, and to inspire fear into all possessed of understanding. But those objects of terror which surpass not the strength of human nature, differing from each other in magnitude, as well as do the grounds of confidence, courage will discriminate between real and apparent dangers; and make us meet the former, as brave men ought, unshaken and dauntless, subjecting the instinctive emotions of fear to the dictates of reason and of honor. For we betray our weakness, not only when we fear things really not formidable, but when we are affected in an undue degree, or at an improper time, by objects of real danger. A brave man avoids such errors; and, estimating things by their real worth, prefers the grace and beauty of habitual fortitude to the delusive security of deformed cowardice. Yet he is not less careful to avoid that excess of intrepidity, which, being rarely met with, is like many other vices, without a name; though nothing but madness, or a most stupid insensibility, can make any man preserve, amidst earthquakes and inundations, that unshaken composure, which has been ascribed to the Celts. An overweening estimate of the causes of confidence, and a consequent excess of courage, is called audacity; a boastful species of bravery, and the mere ape of true manhood. What the brave man *is*, the rash and audacious man wishes to *appear;* he courts and provokes unnecessary dangers, but fails in the hour of trial; and is, for the most part, a blustering bully, who, under a semblance of pretended courage, conceals no inconsiderable portion of cowardice.

But the complete and genuine coward easily betrays himself, by fearing either things not formidable, or things formidable, in an undue degree; and his failing is the more manifest, because it is accompanied with plain indications of pain; he lives in continual alarm, and is therefore spiritless and dejected; whereas courage warms our breasts, and animates our hopes. Such then is the character of true courage, as opposed to audacity on one hand, and cowardice on the other. It holds the middle place between those vicious extremes; it is calm and sedate; and though it never provokes danger, is always ready to meet even death in an honourable cause. But to die, rather than endure manfully the pressure of poverty, or the stings of love, or any other cruel suffering, is the part of a coward; who basely flies from an enemy that he has not spirit to encounter; and ignominiously quits the field, where he might have sustained a strenuous and honourable conflict.

Order of the Day: June 6, 1944
By General Dwight D. Eisenhower

This is the message the Supreme Commander of Europe's Allied Forces, General Dwight D. Eisenhower, gave the 175,000-member expeditionary force before the landing at Normandy during World War II. On June 5, 1944, the day before the invasion, he went to bid farewell to the Allied paratroopers preparing to take flight towards France. He shook the hands of the men of America's 101st Airborne division and then climbed to the roof of a headquarters building to watch the C-47s take flight. Aware that the casualty rate for these men had been predicted to reach as high as 75 percent, he saluted the planes as they tore into the sky, tears filling his eyes.

Soldiers, Sailors and Airmen of the Allied Expeditionary Forces!

You are about to embark upon the Great Crusade, toward which we have striven these many months. The eyes of the world are upon you. The hopes and prayers of liberty-loving people everywhere march with you. In company with our brave Allies and brothers-in-arms on other Fronts you will bring about the destruction of the German war machine, the elimination of Nazi tyranny over the oppressed peoples of Europe, and security for ourselves in a free world.

Your task will not be an easy one. Your enemy is well trained, well equipped and battle-hardened. He will fight savagely.

But this is the year 1944! Much has happened since the Nazi triumphs of 1940–41. The United Nations have inflicted upon the Germans great defeats, in open battle, man-to-man. Our air offensive has seriously reduced their strength in the air and their capacity to wage war on the ground. Our Home Fronts have given us an overwhelming superiority in weapons and munitions of war, and placed at our disposal great reserves of trained fighting men. The tide has turned! The free men of the world are marching together to victory!

I have full confidence in your courage, devotion to duty, and skill in battle. We will accept nothing less than full Victory!

Good Luck! And let us all beseech the blessing of Almighty God upon this great and noble undertaking.

"Brave men are vertebrates; they have their softness on the surface and their toughness in the middle. But these modern cowards are all crustaceans; their hardness is all on the cover and their softness is inside." —G.K. Chesterton

The Courage of His Convictions
FROM *THE STRANDED BUGLE*, 1905
By Leroy E. Mosher

All men of principle and of steadfastness approve the man who has the courage of his convictions. Such a man necessarily makes enemies; but even an enemy entertains a wholesome respect for the man who honestly differs from him and is not afraid to advocate and defend his views upon all proper occasions.

The men of courage, the men of positive ideas, are the men who make history. Without them there would be no progress. The world would retrograde. Civilization would turn backward. The glorious achievements of the past would be wasted, and the future would hold no promise.

It is easier to drift with the current than to oppose it. Those who go counter to accepted ideas often impose upon themselves a thankless and unpleasant task. They incur the reproaches of unjust critics, the contumely of enemies, and too often the ill will of those who are, or should be, their friends. But these things have little weight with the man who is actuated by deep and abiding convictions. He will do his duty as he sees it at all hazards, and in spite of opposition or adverse criticism, leaving to the future the vindication of his action.

The Charge of the Light Brigade
By Alfred, Lord Tennyson, 1854

••

This poem was inspired by a charge made by British cavalry against the Russian army during the Crimean War. Due to a miscommunication, a small band of around six hundred cavalrymen rode into a valley surrounded by twenty Russian battalions armed with heavy artillery. While the British cavalry was resoundingly and tragically defeated, and their commanders sharply criticized for the heavy casualties, the bravery of the men who charged into the "valley of death" was celebrated and honored.

· ·

Half a league half a league,
Half a league onward,
All in the valley of Death
Rode the six hundred:
'Forward, the Light Brigade!
Charge for the guns' he said:
Into the valley of Death
Rode the six hundred.

'Forward, the Light Brigade!'
Was there a man dismay'd?
Not tho' the soldier knew
Some one had blunder'd:
Theirs not to make reply,
Theirs not to reason why,
Theirs but to do & die,
Into the valley of Death
Rode the six hundred.

Cannon to right of them,
Cannon to left of them,
Cannon in front of them
Volley'd & thunder'd;
Storm'd at with shot and shell,
Boldly they rode and well,
Into the jaws of Death,

Into the mouth of Hell
Rode the six hundred.

Flash'd all their sabres bare,
Flash'd as they turn'd in air
Sabring the gunners there,
Charging an army while
All the world wonder'd:
Plunged in the battery-smoke
Right thro' the line they broke;
Cossack & Russian
Reel'd from the sabre-stroke,
Shatter'd & sunder'd.
Then they rode back, but not
Not the six hundred.

Cannon to right of them,
Cannon to left of them,
Cannon behind them

Volley'd and thunder'd;
Storm'd at with shot and shell,
While horse & hero fell,
They that had fought so well
Came thro' the jaws of Death,
Back from the mouth of Hell,
All that was left of them,
Left of six hundred.

When can their glory fade?
O the wild charge they made!
All the world wonder'd.
Honour the charge they made!
Honour the Light Brigade,
Noble six hundred!

"Courage is a moral quality; it is not a chance gift of nature like an aptitude for games. It is a cold choice between two alternatives, the fixed resolve not to quit; an act of renunciation which must be made not once but many times by the power of the will. Courage is willpower." —Lord Moran

A classified ad said to have been placed in a London newspaper by Ernest Shackleton, explorer of the Antarctic, before his Nimrod expedition in 1908.

MEN WANTED

FOR HAZARDOUS JOURNEY. Small wages, bitter cold, long months of complete darkness, constant danger, safe return doubtful. Honor and recognition in case of success.

"All brave men love; for he only is brave who has affections to fight for, whether in the daily battle of life, or in physical contests." —*Nathaniel Hawthorne*

Why Direct Action?

FROM "LETTER FROM BIRMINGHAM JAIL," 1963
By Martin Luther King Jr.

In the spring of 1963, Martin Luther King Jr. and the Southern Christian Leadership Conference staged a civil rights campaign in Birmingham, Alabama. Using non-violent, direct action tactics such as marches and sit-ins, activists sought to bring national attention to the discrimination in what was then considered the most segregated city in America. Protestors, including King, who ignored the city's injunction against the campaign were jailed in mass arrests. When eight white Alabama clergymen issued a statement which criticized the Birmingham campaign for stirring up unrest and called for a more patient, slower approach to gaining civil rights, King penned this open letter, passionately defending his methods, explaining the need to move forward, and arguing that breaking unjust laws constituted an act of great moral courage.

16 April 1963

My Dear Fellow Clergymen:

While confined here in the Birmingham City Jail, I came across your recent statement calling my present activities "unwise and untimely." Seldom do I pause to answer criticism of my work and ideas. … But since I feel that you are men of genuine good will and that your criticisms are sincerely set forth, I want to try to answer your statement in what I hope will be patient and reasonable terms.

You may well ask: "Why direct action? Why sit-ins, marches and so forth? Isn't negotiation a better path?" You are quite right in calling for negotiation. Indeed, this is the very purpose of direct action. Nonviolent direct action seeks to create such a crisis and foster such a tension that a community which has constantly refused to negotiate is forced to confront the issue. It seeks so to dramatize the issue that it can no longer be ignored. My citing the creation of tension as part of the work of the nonviolent-resister may sound rather shocking. But I must confess that I am not afraid of the word "tension." I have earnestly opposed violent tension, but there is a type of constructive, nonviolent tension which is necessary for growth. Just as Socrates felt that it was necessary to create a tension in the mind so that individuals could rise from the bondage of myths and half-truths to the unfettered realm of creative analysis and objective appraisal, so must we see the need for nonviolent gadflies to create the kind of tension in society that will help men rise from the dark depths of prejudice and racism to the majestic heights of understanding and brotherhood.

The purpose of our direct-action program is to create a situation so crisis-packed that it will inevitably open the door to negotiation. I therefore concur with you in your call for negotiation. Too long has our beloved Southland been bogged down in a tragic effort to live in monologue rather than dialogue.

One of the basic points in your statement is that the action that I and my associates have taken in Birmingham is untimely. Some have asked: "Why didn't you give the new city administration time to act?" ... My friends, I must say to you that we have not made a single gain in civil rights without determined legal and nonviolent pressure. Lamentably, it is an historical fact that privileged groups seldom give up their privileges voluntarily. Individuals may see the moral light and voluntarily give up their unjust posture; but, as Reinhold Niebuhr has reminded us, groups tend to be more immoral than individuals.

We know through painful experience that freedom is never voluntarily given by the oppressor; it must be demanded by the oppressed. Frankly, I have yet to engage in a direct-action campaign that was "well timed" in the view of those who have not suffered unduly from the disease of segregation. For years now I have heard the word "Wait!" It rings in the ear of every Negro with piercing familiarity. This "Wait" has almost always meant "Never." We must come to see, with one of our distinguished jurists, that "justice too long delayed is justice denied."

We have waited for more than 340 years for our constitutional and God given rights. The nations of Asia and Africa are moving with jet-like speed toward gaining political independence, but we still creep at horse and buggy pace toward gaining a cup of coffee at a lunch counter. Perhaps it is easy for those who have never felt the stinging darts of segregation to say, "Wait." But when you have seen vicious mobs lynch your mothers and fathers at will and drown your sisters and brothers at whim; when you have seen hate filled policemen curse, kick and even kill your black brothers and sisters; when you see the vast majority of your twenty million Negro brothers smothering in an airtight cage of poverty in the midst of an affluent society; when you suddenly find your tongue twisted and your speech stammering as you seek to explain to your six year old daughter why she can't go to the public amusement park that has just been advertised on television, and see tears welling up in her eyes when she is told that Funtown is closed to colored children, and see ominous clouds of inferiority beginning to form in her little mental sky, and see her beginning to distort her personality by developing an unconscious bitterness toward white people; when you have to concoct an answer for a five year old son who is asking: "Daddy, why do white people treat colored people so mean?"; when you take a cross county drive and find it necessary to sleep night after night in the uncomfortable corners of your automobile because no motel will accept you; when you are humiliated day in and day out by nagging signs reading "white" and "colored"; when your first name becomes "nigger," your middle name becomes "boy" (however old you are) and your last name becomes "John," and your wife and mother are never given the respected title "Mrs."; when you are harried by day and haunted by night by the fact that you are a Negro, living constantly at tiptoe stance, never quite knowing what to expect next, and are plagued with inner fears and outer resentments; when you are forever fighting a degenerating sense of "nobodiness"—then you will understand why we find it difficult to wait. There comes a time when the cup of endurance runs over, and men are no longer willing to be plunged into the abyss of despair. I hope, sirs, you can understand our legitimate and unavoidable impatience. You express a great deal of anxiety over our willingness to break laws. This is certainly a legitimate concern. Since we so diligently urge people to obey the Supreme Court's decision of 1954 outlawing segregation in the public schools, at first glance it may seem rather paradoxical for us consciously to break laws. One may well ask: "How can you advocate breaking some laws and obeying others?" The answer lies in the fact that there are two types of laws: just and unjust. I would be the first to advocate obeying just laws. One has not only a legal but a moral responsibility to obey just laws. Conversely, one has a moral responsibility to disobey unjust laws. I would agree with St. Augustine that "an unjust law is no law at all."

Now, what is the difference between the two? How does one determine whether a law is just or unjust? A just law is a man made code that squares with the moral law or the law of God. An unjust law is a code that is out of harmony with the moral law. To put it in the terms of St. Thomas Aquinas: An unjust law is a human law that is not rooted in eternal law and natural law. Any law that uplifts human personality is just. Any law that degrades human personality is unjust. All segregation statutes are unjust because segregation distorts the soul and damages the personality. It gives the segregator a false sense of superiority and the segregated a false sense of inferiority. Segregation, to use the terminology of the Jewish philosopher Martin Buber, substitutes an "I it" relationship for an

"I thou" relationship and ends up relegating persons to the status of things. Hence segregation is not only politically, economically and sociologically unsound, it is morally wrong and sinful. Paul Tillich has said that sin is separation. Is not segregation an existential expression of man's tragic separation, his awful estrangement, his terrible sinfulness? Thus it is that I can urge men to obey the 1954 decision of the Supreme Court, for it is morally right; and I can urge them to disobey segregation ordinances, for they are morally wrong.

In no sense do I advocate evading or defying the law, as would the rabid segregationist. That would lead to anarchy. One who breaks an unjust law must do so openly, lovingly, and with a willingness to accept the penalty. I submit that an individual who breaks a law that conscience tells him is unjust, and who willingly accepts the penalty of imprisonment in order to arouse the conscience of the community over its injustice, is in reality expressing the highest respect for law.

Of course, there is nothing new about this kind of civil disobedience. It was evidenced sublimely in the refusal of Shadrach, Meshach and Abednego to obey the laws of Nebuchadnezzar, on the ground that a higher moral law was at stake. It was practiced superbly by the early Christians, who were willing to face hungry lions and the excruciating pain of chopping blocks rather than submit to certain unjust laws of the Roman Empire. To a degree, academic freedom is a reality today because Socrates practiced civil disobedience. In our own nation, the Boston Tea Party represented a massive act of civil disobedience.

We should never forget that everything Adolf Hitler did in Germany was "legal" and everything the Hungarian freedom fighters did in Hungary was "illegal." It was "illegal" to aid and comfort a Jew in Hitler's Germany. Even so, I am sure that, had I lived in Germany at the time, I would have aided and comforted my Jewish brothers. If today I lived in a Communist country where certain principles dear to the Christian faith are suppressed, I would openly advocate disobeying that country's antireligious laws.

So I have not said to my people: "Get rid of your discontent." Rather, I have tried to say that this normal and healthy discontent can be channeled into the creative outlet of nonviolent direct action. And now this approach is being termed extremist. But though I was initially disappointed at being categorized as an extremist, as I continued to think about the matter I gradually gained a measure of satisfaction from the label. Was not Jesus an extremist for love: "Love your enemies, bless them that curse you, do good to them that hate you, and pray for them which despitefully use you, and persecute you." Was not Amos an extremist for justice: "Let justice roll down like waters and righteousness like an ever flowing stream." Was not Paul an extremist for the Christian gospel: "I bear in my body the marks of the Lord Jesus." Was not Martin Luther an extremist: "Here I stand; I cannot do otherwise, so help me God." And John Bunyan: "I will stay in jail to the end of my days before I make a butchery of my conscience." And Abraham Lincoln: "This nation cannot survive half slave and half free." And Thomas Jefferson: "We hold these truths to be self evident, that all men are created equal …" So the question is not whether we will be extremists, but what kind of extremists we will be. Will we be extremists for hate or for love? Will we be extremists for the preservation of injustice or for the extension of justice? … Perhaps the South, the nation and the world are in dire need of creative extremists.

I wish you had commended the Negro sit inners and demonstrators of Birmingham for their sublime courage, their willingness to suffer and their amazing discipline in the midst of great provocation. One day the South will recognize its real heroes. They will be the James Merediths, with the noble sense of purpose that enables them to face jeering and hostile mobs, and with the agonizing loneliness that characterizes the life of the pioneer. They will be old, oppressed, battered Negro women, symbolized in a seventy two year old woman in Montgomery, Alabama, who rose up with a sense of dignity and with her people decided not to ride segregated buses, and who responded with ungrammatical profundity to one who inquired about her weariness: "My feets is tired, but my soul is at rest." They will be the young high school and college students, the young ministers of the gospel and a host of their elders, courageously and nonviolently sitting in at lunch counters and willingly going to jail for conscience' sake. One day the South will know that when these disinherited children of God sat down at lunch counters, they were in reality standing up for what is best in the American dream and for the most sacred values in our Judaeo Christian heritage, thereby bringing our nation back to those great wells of democracy which were dug deep by the founding fathers in their formulation of the Constitution and the Declaration of Independence.

Yours for the cause of Peace and Brotherhood, Martin Luther King, Jr.

> *"The courage we desire and prize is not the courage to die decently, but to live manfully."* —Thomas Carlyle

Self-Trust Is the Essence of Heroism
FROM THE ESSAY "HEROISM," IN *ESSAYS, FIRST SERIES*, 1841
By Ralph Waldo Emerson

Self-trust is the essence of heroism. It is the state of the soul at war, and its ultimate objects are the last defiance of falsehood and wrong, and the power to bear all that can be inflicted by evil agents. It speaks the truth, and it is just, generous, hospitable, temperate, scornful of petty calculations, and scornful of being scorned. It persists; it is of an undaunted boldness, and of a fortitude not to be wearied out. Its jest is the littleness of common life. That false prudence which dotes on health and wealth is the butt and merriment of heroism. Heroism, like

Plotinus, is almost ashamed of its body. What shall it say, then, to the sugarplums and cats'-cradles, to the toilet, compliments, quarrels, cards, and custard, which rack the wit of all society. What joys has kind nature provided for us dear creatures! There seems to be no interval between greatness and meanness. When the spirit is not master of the world, then it is its dupe. Yet the little man takes the great hoax so innocently, works in it so headlong and believing, is born red, and dies gray, arranging his toilet, attending on his own health, laying traps for sweet food and strong wine, setting his heart on a horse or a rifle, made happy with a little gossip or a little praise, that the great soul cannot choose but laugh at such earnest nonsense. "Indeed, these humble considerations make me out of love with greatness. What a disgrace is it to me to take note how many pairs of silk stockings thou hast, namely, these and those that were the peach-colored ones; or to bear the inventory of thy shirts, as one for superfluity, and one other for use!"

The characteristic of heroism is its persistency. All men have wandering impulses, fits, and starts of generosity. But when you have chosen your part, abide by it, and do not weakly try to reconcile yourself with the world. The heroic cannot be the common, nor the common the heroic. Yet we have the weakness to expect the sympathy of people in those actions whose excellence is that they outrun sympathy, and appeal to a tardy justice. If you would serve your brother, because it is fit for you to serve him, do not take back your words when you find that prudent people do not commend you. Adhere to your own act, and congratulate yourself if you have done something strange and extravagant, and broken the monotony of a decorous age. It was a high counsel that I once heard given to a young person— "Always do what you are afraid to do."

"True courage is not the brutal force of vulgar heroes. Rather the firm resolve of virtue and reason." —Alfred North Whitehead

Duty, Honor, Country

FROM A SPEECH, 1962
By General Douglas MacArthur

Douglas MacArthur served in the US Army for fifty-two years, most famously as General and then Supreme Commander of the Allied Powers during World War II. Nearing the end of his life, he returned to his alma mater, West Point, to receive the Sylvanus Thayer Award, given to those who render outstanding service to the nation and embody the Academy's motto of "Duty, Honor, Country." Focusing on that theme, MacArthur made the following remarks to the Corps of Cadets upon accepting the award.

Duty, Honor, Country: Those three hallowed words reverently dictate what you ought to be, what you can be, what you will be. They are your rallying points: to build courage when courage seems to fail; to regain faith when there seems to be little cause for faith; to create hope when hope becomes forlorn.

The unbelievers will say they are but words, but a slogan, but a flamboyant phrase. Every pedant, every demagogue, every cynic, every hypocrite, every troublemaker, and, I am sorry to say, some others of an entirely different character, will try to downgrade them even to the extent of mockery and ridicule.

But these are some of the things they do. They build your basic character. They mold you for your future roles as the custodians of the nation's defense. They make you strong enough to know when you are weak, and brave enough to face yourself when you are afraid.

COURAGE

They teach you to be proud and unbending in honest failure, but humble and gentle in success; not to substitute words for action; not to seek the path of comfort, but to face the stress and spur of difficulty and challenge; to learn to stand up in the storm, but to have compassion on those who fall; to master yourself before you seek to master others; to have a heart that is clean, a goal that is high; to learn to laugh, yet never forget how to weep; to reach into the future, yet never neglect the past; to be serious, yet never take yourself too seriously; to be modest so that you will remember the simplicity of true greatness; the open mind of true wisdom, the meekness of true strength.

They give you a temperate will, a quality of imagination, a vigor of the emotions, a freshness of the deep springs of life, a temperamental predominance of courage over timidity, an appetite for adventure over love of ease. They create in your heart the sense of wonder, the unfailing hope of what next, and the joy and inspiration of life. They teach you in this way to be an officer and a gentleman.

And what sort of soldiers are those you are to lead? Are they reliable? Are they brave? Are they capable of victory?

Their story is known to all of you. It is the story of the American man at arms. My estimate of him was formed on the battlefields many, many years ago, and has never changed. I regarded him then, as I regard him now, as one of the world's noblest figures; not only as one of the finest military characters, but also as one of the most stainless.

His name and fame are the birthright of every American citizen. In his youth and strength, his love and loyalty, he gave all that mortality can give. He needs no eulogy from me, or from any other man. He has written his own history and written it in red on his enemy's breast.

But when I think of his patience under adversity, of his courage under fire, and of his modesty in victory, I am filled with an emotion of admiration I cannot put into words. He belongs to history as furnishing one of the greatest examples of successful patriotism. He belongs to posterity as the

CHAPTER TWO

instructor of future generations in the principles of liberty and freedom. He belongs to the present, to us, by his virtues and by his achievements.

In twenty campaigns, on a hundred battlefields, around a thousand campfires, I have witnessed that enduring fortitude, that patriotic self-abnegation, and that invincible determination which have carved his statue in the hearts of his people.

From one end of the world to the other, he has drained deep the chalice of courage. As I listened to those songs of the glee club, in memory's eye I could see those staggering columns of the First World War, bending under soggy packs on many a weary march, from dripping dusk to drizzling dawn, slogging ankle deep through mire of shell-pocked roads; to form grimly for the attack, blue-lipped, covered with sludge and mud, chilled by the wind and rain, driving home to their objective, and for many, to the judgment seat of God.

I do not know the dignity of their birth, but I do know the glory of their death. They died unquestioning, uncomplaining, with faith in their hearts, and on their lips the hope that we would go on to victory. Always for them: Duty, Honor, Country. Always their blood, and sweat, and tears, as they saw the way and the light.

And twenty years after, on the other side of the globe, against the filth of dirty foxholes, the stench of ghostly trenches, the slime of dripping dugouts, those boiling suns of the relentless heat, those torrential rains of devastating storms, the loneliness and utter desolation of jungle trails, the bitterness of long separation of those they loved and cherished, the deadly pestilence of tropic disease, the horror of stricken areas of war.

Their resolute and determined defense, their swift and sure attack, their indomitable purpose, their complete and decisive victory—always victory, always through the bloody haze of their last reverberating shot, the vision of gaunt, ghastly men, reverently following your password of Duty, Honor, Country.

The code which those words perpetuate embraces the highest moral laws and will stand the test of any ethics or philosophies ever promulgated for the uplift of mankind. Its requirements are for the things that are right, and its restraints are from the things that are wrong. The soldier, above all other men, is required to practice the greatest act of religious training—sacrifice. In battle and in the face of danger and death, he discloses those divine attributes which his Maker gave when he created man in his own image. No physical courage and no brute instinct can take the place of the Divine help which alone can sustain him. However horrible the incidents of war may be, the soldier who is called upon to offer and to give his life for his country, is the noblest development of mankind.

The long gray line has never failed us. Were you to do so, a million ghosts in olive drab, in brown khaki, in blue and gray, would rise from their white crosses, thundering those magic words: Duty, Honor, Country.

This does not mean that you are warmongers. On the contrary, the soldier above all other people prays for peace, for he must suffer and bear the deepest wounds and scars of war. But always in our ears ring the ominous words of Plato, that wisest of all philosophers: "Only the dead have seen the end of war."

The shadows are lengthening for me. The twilight is here. My days of old have vanished—tone and tints. They have gone glimmering through the dreams of things that were. Their memory is one of wondrous beauty, watered by tears and coaxed and caressed by the smiles of yesterday. I listen then, but with thirsty ear, for the witching melody of faint bugles blowing reveille, of far drums beating the long roll.

In my dreams I hear again the crash of guns, the rattle of musketry, the strange, mournful mutter of the battlefield. But in the evening of my memory I come back to West Point. Always there echoes and re-echoes: Duty, Honor, Country.

"Courage is not simply one of the virtues, but the form of every virtue at the testing point." —C.S. Lewis

Heroes

FROM "SONG OF MYSELF," 1855
By Walt Whitman

I understand the large hearts of heroes,

The courage of present times and all times,

How the skipper saw the crowded and rudderless wreck of the steam-
ship, and Death chasing it up and down the storm,

How he knuckled tight and gave not back an inch, and was faithful of
days and faithful of nights,

And chalk'd in large letters on a board, *Be of good cheer, we will not
desert you*;

How he follow'd with them and tack'd with them three days and would
not give it up,

How he saved the drifting company at last,

How the lank loose-gown'd women look'd when boated from the side of
their prepared graves,

How the silent old-faced infants and the lifted sick, and the sharp-lipp'd
unshaved men;

All this I swallow, it tastes good, I like it well, it becomes mine,
I am the man, I suffer'd, I was there.

*"Courage is contagious. When a brave man takes a stand, the
spines of others are often stiffened."* —Billy Graham

The Hunter and the Woodsman
An Aesop's Fable

A hunter, not very bold, was searching for the tracks of a Lion. He asked a
man felling oaks in the forest if he had seen any marks of his footsteps, or
if he knew where his lair was. "I will," he said, "at once show you the Lion
himself." The Hunter, turning very pale, and chattering with his teeth from
fear, replied, "No, thank you. I did not ask that; it is his track only I am in
search of, not the Lion himself."

The hero is brave in deeds as well as words.

*"Courage is resistance to fear, mastery of fear—not absence of
fear. Except a creature be part coward, it is not a compliment to
say it is brave; it is merely a loose misapplication of the word.
Consider the flea!—incomparably the bravest of all the creatures of God, if ignorance of fear were courage."* —Mark Twain

Fighting
From *Tom Brown's School Days*, 1857
By Thomas Hughes

Tom Brown's School Days was a popular nineteenth-century novel that followed
eleven-year-old Tom Brown, as he adjusted to life at a public boarding school

for boys and learned how to become a young gentleman. The following excerpts refer to Tom's only big fight at the school. The headmaster had given him a student to look after, and when a large bully attacked the frail and sensitive boy, Tom stepped in to stop the beating and fight the bully himself.

After all, what would life be without fighting, I should like to know? From the cradle to the grave, fighting, rightly understood, is the business, the real, highest, honestest business of every son of man. Every one who is worth his salt has his enemies, who must be beaten, be they evil thoughts and habits in himself or spiritual wickedness in high places, or Russians, or Border-ruffians, or Bill, Tom, or Harry, who will not let him live his life in quiet till he has thrashed them.

It is no good for Quakers, or any other body of men, to uplift their voices against fighting. Human nature is too strong for them, and they don't follow their own precepts. Every soul of them is doing his own piece of fighting, somehow and somewhere. The world might be a better world without fighting, for anything I know, but it wouldn't be our world; and therefore I am dead against crying peace when there is no peace, and isn't meant to be. I'm as sorry as any man to see folk fighting the wrong people and the wrong things, but I'd a deal sooner see them doing that, than that they should have no fight in them.

———•———

As to fighting, keep out of it if you can, by all means. When the time comes, if it ever should, that you have to say "Yes" or "No" to a challenge to fight, say "No" if you can—only take care you make it clear to yourselves why you say "No." It's a proof of the highest courage, if done from true Christian motives. It's quite right and justifiable, if done from a simple aversion to physical pain and danger. But don't say "No" because you fear a licking, and say or think it's because you fear God, for that's neither Christian nor honest. And if you do fight, fight it out; and don't give in while you can stand and see.

"Live as brave men and face adversity with stout hearts." —Horace

Horatius
From *Lays of Ancient Rome*, 1842
By Thomas Babington Macaulay

· ·

While serving the English government in India during the 1830s, politician, poet, and historian Thomas Babington Macaulay spun semi-mythical ancient Roman tales into memorable ballads or "lays." His most famous lay was "Horatius," a ballad that recounted the legendary courage of an ancient Roman army officer, Publius Horatius Cocles. In the fifth century B.C., Rome rebelled against Etruscan rule and ousted their last king, Lucius Tarquinius Superbus, to form a republic. But the king refused to go quietly into the night; he enlisted the help of Lars Porsena of Clusium in an attempt to overthrow the new Roman government and re-establish his reign.

In a battle against the approaching Etruscans, the Roman army faced defeat and began to retreat across the bridge which traversed the Tiber River. And this is where we'll let the poem pick up the heroic tale.

Manly factoid: "Horatius" was a favorite of Winston Churchill who is said to have memorized all seventy stanzas of the poem as a boy (we've included thirty-four of them here).

• •

And nearer fast and nearer
Doth the red whirlwind come;
And louder still and still more loud,
From underneath that rolling cloud,
Is heard the trumpet's war-note proud,
The trampling, and the hum.
And plainly and more plainly
Now through the gloom appears,
Far to left and far to right,
In broken gleams of dark-blue light,
The long array of helmets bright,
The long array of spears.

Fast by the royal standard,
O'erlooking all the war,
Lars Porsena of Clusium
Sat in his ivory car.
By the right wheel rode Mamilius,
Prince of the Latian name;
And by the left false Sextus,
That wrought the deed of shame.

But when the face of Sextus
Was seen among the foes,

A yell that rent the firmament
From all the town arose.
On the house-tops was no woman
But spat towards him and hissed;
No child but screamed out curses,
And shook its little fist.

But the Consul's brow was sad,
And the Consul's speech was low,
And darkly looked he at the wall,
And darkly at the foe.
"Their van will be upon us
Before the bridge goes down;
And if they once may win the bridge,
What hope to save the town?"

Then out spake brave Horatius,
The Captain of the Gate:
"To every man upon this earth
Death cometh soon or late.
And how can man die better
Than facing fearful odds,
For the ashes of his fathers,
And the temples of his gods,

"And for the tender mother
Who dandled him to rest,
And for the wife who nurses
His baby at her breast,
And for the holy maidens
Who feed the eternal flame,
To save them from false Sextus
That wrought the deed of shame?

"Haul down the bridge, Sir Consul,
  With all the speed ye may;
  I, with two more to help me,
  Will hold the foe in play.
  In yon strait path a thousand
  May well be stopped by three.
  Now who will stand on either hand,
  And keep the bridge with me?"

Then out spake Spurius Lartius;
  A Ramnian proud was he:
"Lo, I will stand at thy right hand,
  And keep the bridge with thee."
And out spake strong Herminius;
  Of Titian blood was he:
"I will abide on thy left side,
  And keep the bridge with thee."

"Horatius," quoth the Consul,
"As thou sayest, so let it be."
  And straight against that great array
  Forth went the dauntless Three.
  For Romans in Rome's quarrel
  Spared neither land nor gold,
  Nor son nor wife, nor limb nor life,
  In the brave days of old.

Now while the Three were tightening
  Their harness on their backs,
  The Consul was the foremost man
  To take in hand an axe:
  And Fathers mixed with Commons
  Seized hatchet, bar, and crow,

And smote upon the planks above,
And loosed the props below.

Meanwhile the Tuscan army,
Right glorious to behold,
Come flashing back the noonday light,
Rank behind rank, like surges bright
Of a broad sea of gold.
Four hundred trumpets sounded
A peal of warlike glee,
As that great host, with measured tread,
And spears advanced, and ensigns spread,
Rolled slowly towards the bridge's head,
Where stood the dauntless Three.

The Three stood calm and silent,
And looked upon the foes,
And a great shout of laughter
From all the vanguard rose:
And forth three chiefs came spurring
Before that deep array;
To earth they sprang, their swords they drew,
And lifted high their shields, and flew
To win the narrow way;

Aunus from green Tifernum,
Lord of the Hill of Vines;
And Seius, whose eight hundred slaves
Sicken in Ilva's mines;
And Picus, long to Clusium
Vassal in peace and war,
Who led to fight his Umbrian powers
From that gray crag where, girt with towers,

The fortress of Nequinum lowers
O'er the pale waves of Nar.

Stout Lartius hurled down Aunus
Into the stream beneath;
Herminius struck at Seius,
And clove him to the teeth;
At Picus brave Horatius
Darted one fiery thrust;
And the proud Umbrian's gilded arms
Clashed in the bloody dust.

Then Ocnus of Falerii
Rushed on the Roman Three;
And Lausulus of Urgo,
The rover of the sea;

And Aruns of Volsinium,
Who slew the great wild boar,
The great wild boar that had his den
Amidst the reeds of Cosa's fen,
And wasted fields, and slaughtered men,
Along Albinia's shore.

Herminius smote down Aruns:
Lartius laid Ocnus low:
Right to the heart of Lausulus
Horatius sent a blow.
"Lie there," he cried, "fell pirate!
No more, aghast and pale,
From Ostia's walls the crowd shall mark
The track of thy destroying bark.
No more Campania's hinds shall fly
To woods and caverns when they spy
Thy thrice accursed sail."

But now no sound of laughter
Was heard among the foes.
A wild and wrathful clamor
From all the vanguard rose.
Six spears' lengths from the entrance
Halted that deep array,
And for a space no man came forth
To win the narrow way.

But all Etruria's noblest
Felt their hearts sink to see
On the earth the bloody corpses,
In the path the dauntless Three:
And, from the ghastly entrance

Where those bold Romans stood,
All shrank, like boys who unaware,
Ranging the woods to start a hare,
Come to the mouth of the dark lair
Where, growling low, a fierce old bear
Lies amidst bones and blood.

Yet one man for one moment
  Strode out before the crowd;
Well known was he to all the Three,
And they gave him greeting loud.
"Now welcome, welcome, Sextus!
  Now welcome to thy home!
Why dost thou stay, and turn away?
  Here lies the road to Rome."

Thrice looked he at the city;
  Thrice looked he at the dead;
And thrice came on in fury,
  And thrice turned back in dread:
And, white with fear and hatred,
  Scowled at the narrow way
Where, wallowing in a pool of blood,
  The bravest Tuscans lay.

But meanwhile axe and lever
  Have manfully been plied;
And now the bridge hangs tottering
  Above the boiling tide.
"Come back, come back, Horatius!"
  Loud cried the Fathers all.
"Back, Lartius! Back, Herminius!
  Back, ere the ruin fall!"

Back darted Spurius Lartius;
Herminius darted back:
And, as they passed, beneath their feet
They felt the timbers crack.
But when they turned their faces,
And on the farther shore
Saw brave Horatius stand alone,
They would have crossed once more.

But with a crash like thunder
Fell every loosened beam,
And, like a dam, the mighty wreck
Lay right athwart the stream:
And a long shout of triumph
Rose from the walls of Rome,
As to the highest turret-tops
Was splashed the yellow foam.

And, like a horse unbroken
When first he feels the rein,
The furious river struggled hard,
And tossed his tawny mane,
And burst the curb and bounded,
Rejoicing to be free,
And whirling down, in fierce career,
Battlement, and plank, and pier,
Rushed headlong to the sea.

Alone stood brave Horatius,
But constant still in mind;
Thrice thirty thousand foes before,
And the broad flood behind.
"Down with him!" cried false Sextus,

With a smile on his pale face.
"Now yield thee," cried Lars Porsena,
"Now yield thee to our grace."

Round turned he, as not deigning
Those craven ranks to see;
Nought spake he to Lars Porsena,
To Sextus nought spake he;
But he saw on Palatinus
The white porch of his home;
And he spake to the noble river
That rolls by the towers of Rome.

"Oh, Tiber! Father Tiber!
To whom the Romans pray,
A Roman's life, a Roman's arms,
Take thou in charge this day!"
So he spake, and speaking sheathed
The good sword by his side,
And with his harness on his back,
Plunged headlong in the tide.

No sound of joy or sorrow
Was heard from either bank;
But friends and foes in dumb surprise,
With parted lips and straining eyes,
Stood gazing where he sank;
And when above the surges,
They saw his crest appear,
All Rome sent forth a rapturous cry,
And even the ranks of Tuscany
Could scarce forbear to cheer.

But fiercely ran the current,
Swollen high by months of rain:
And fast his blood was flowing;
And he was sore in pain,
And heavy with his armor,
And spent with changing blows:
And oft they thought him sinking,
But still again he rose.

Never, I ween, did swimmer,
In such an evil case,
Struggle through such a raging flood
Safe to the landing place:
But his limbs were borne up bravely
By the brave heart within,
And our good father Tiber
Bare bravely up his chin.

"Curse on him!" quoth false Sextus;
"Will not the villain drown?
But for this stay, ere close of day
We should have sacked the town!"
"Heaven help him!" quoth Lars Porsena
"And bring him safe to shore;
For such a gallant feat of arms
Was never seen before."

And now he feels the bottom;
Now on dry earth he stands;
Now round him throng the Fathers;
To press his gory hands;
And now, with shouts and clapping,
And noise of weeping loud,

He enters through the River-Gate
Borne by the joyous crowd.

They gave him of the corn-land,
That was of public right,
As much as two strong oxen
Could plough from morn till night;
And they made a molten image,
And set it up on high,
And there it stands unto this day
To witness if I lie.

It stands in the Comitium
Plain for all folk to see;
Horatius in his harness,
Halting upon one knee:
And underneath is written,
In letters all of gold,
How valiantly he kept the bridge
In the brave days of old.

CHAPTER THREE

INDUSTRY

Is greatness born or made? Despite the myth of mystical innate genius, researchers have found that it's actually the latter. And how is it made? Through hustle and hard work: by harnessing the supreme power of industry.

We have no control over the circumstances into which we are born. But there are two things over which every man has complete sovereignty: time and toil. Every man, rich or poor, has twenty-four hours in a day and seven days in a week to labor as much as he will. Industry and time: these are the great equalizers among men. And how they are used is what separates the mediocre from the extraordinary.

The world's greatest men understood this principle; they knew they had a limited amount of time on this planet to make their mark. They understood that glory and honor go to the man who uses his time wisely and effectively, and so they got to work.

Take Theodore Roosevelt for example. In his sixty-year life, he served as state legislator, police commissioner, governor of New York, and president of the United States, penned over thirty-five books and read tens of thousands of them, owned and worked his own cattle ranch, formed a cavalry unit to fight in the Spanish-American War, navigated an uncharted Amazonian river, and became the first American to win the Nobel Prize.

Benjamin Franklin was another great man who accomplished much during his life. From humble beginnings as the son of a candlemaker, he became a successful printer, inventor, writer, scientist, and diplomat. He invented the lightning rod, bifocal glasses, swim fins, and a more efficient wood-burning stove. He conducted scientific experiments and inquiries into electricity, oceanography, meteorology, temperature, and light. He composed music and played the guitar, violin, and harp. He established the first public library, post office, and fire department in the United States. Oh, and in his spare time, he helped found a country.

Achievement at these awe-inspiring levels may seem impossible to the modern man, who is apt to think these men were simply of an entirely different breed. But Franklin and Roosevelt did not have special powers; whatever innate intelligence they may have been born with would have remained latent if not for their own dogged lifelong pursuit of self-education. No, the secret of their success was really quite simple. They sucked the marrow out of every minute of every single day. They had aim, purpose, and drive. They took every opportunity that came their way and created them when they didn't. They woke up early and attacked the day's work with vim and vigor. They were industry personified.

Each and every day we are creating our legacy. What will you be able to look back on when you're eighty-five? A business started? A book written? A library consumed? A language learned? A child raised? Or vast expanses of time on which the mind draws a blank, an unaccounted for wasteland of life that somehow slipped through the fingers? Better get to work.

Carpe Diem.

• •

"Pereunt et imputantur." ("The hours perish, and are laid to our charge.") —Inscription on a sun dial at Oxford

The Supply of Time
FROM *HOW TO LIVE ON 24 HOURS A DAY*, 1910
By Arnold Bennett

Newspapers are full of articles explaining how to live on such-and-such a sum, and these articles provoke a correspondence whose violence proves

HORAE PEREUNT ET
IMPUTANTUR

the interest they excite. … I have seen an essay, "How to live on eight shillings a week." But I have never seen an essay, "How to live on twenty-four hours a day." Yet it has been said that time is money. That proverb understates the case. Time is a great deal more than money. If you have time you can obtain money—usually. But though you have the wealth of a cloak-room attendant at the Carlton Hotel, you cannot buy yourself a minute more time than I have, or the cat by the fire has.

Philosophers have explained space. They have not explained time. It is the inexplicable raw material of everything. With it, all is possible; without it, nothing. The supply of time is truly a daily miracle, an affair genuinely astonishing when one examines it. You wake up in the morning, and lo! your purse is magically filled with twenty-four hours of the unmanufactured tissue of the universe of your life! It is yours. It is the most precious of possessions. A highly singular commodity, showered upon you in a manner as singular as the commodity itself!

For remark! No one can take it from you. It is unstealable. And no one receives either more or less than you receive.

Talk about an ideal democracy! In the realm of time there is no aristocracy of wealth, and no aristocracy of intellect. Genius is never rewarded by even an extra hour a day. And there is no punishment. Waste your infinitely precious commodity as much as you will, and the supply will never be withheld from you. No mysterious power will say: "This man is a fool, if not a knave. He does not deserve time; he shall be cut off at the meter."

It is more certain than consols, and payment of income is not affected by Sundays. Moreover, you cannot draw on the future. Impossible to get into debt! You can only waste the passing moment. You cannot waste tomorrow; it is kept for you. You cannot waste the next hour; it is kept for you.

I said the affair was a miracle. Is it not?

You have to live on this twenty-four hours of daily time. Out of it you have to spin health, pleasure, money, content, respect, and the evolution of your immortal soul. Its right use, its most effective use, is a matter of the highest urgency and of the most thrilling actuality. All depends on that. Your happiness—the elusive prize that you are all clutching for, my friends!—depends on that. Strange that the newspapers, so enterprising and up-to-date as they are, are not full of "How to live on a given income of time," instead of "How to live on a given income of money!" Money is far commoner than time. When one reflects, one perceives that money is just about the commonest thing there is. It encumbers the earth in gross heaps.

If one can't contrive to live on a certain income of money, one earns a little more—or steals it, or advertises for it. One doesn't necessarily muddle one's life because one can't quite manage on a thousand pounds a year; one braces the muscles and makes it guineas, and balances the budget. But if one cannot arrange that an income of twenty-four hours a day shall exactly cover all proper items of expenditure, one does muddle one's life definitely. The supply of time, though gloriously regular, is cruelly restricted.

Which of us lives on twenty-four hours a day? And when I say "lives," I do not mean exists, nor "muddles through." Which of us is free from that uneasy feeling that the "great spending departments" of his daily life are not managed as they ought to be? … Which of us is not saying to himself—which of us has not been saying to himself all his life: "I shall alter that when I have a little more time?"

Innumerable band of souls who are haunted, more or less painfully, by the feeling that the years slip by, and slip by, and slip by, and that they have not yet been able to get their lives into proper working order.

If we analyse that feeling, we shall perceive it to be, primarily, one of uneasiness, of expectation, of looking forward, of aspiration. It is a source of constant discomfort, for it behaves like a skeleton at the feast of all our enjoyments. We go to the theatre and laugh; but between the acts it raises a skinny finger at us. We rush violently for the last train, and while we are cooling a long age on the platform waiting for the last train, it promenades its bones up and down by our side and inquires: "O man, what hast thou done with thy youth? What art thou doing with thine age?" You may urge that this feeling of continuous looking forward, of aspiration, is part of life itself, and inseparable from life itself. True!

But there are degrees. A man may desire to go to Mecca. His conscience tells him that he ought to go to Mecca. He fares forth, either by the aid of Cook's, or unassisted; he may probably never reach Mecca; he may drown before he gets to Port Said; he may perish ingloriously on the coast of the Red Sea; his desire may remain eternally frustrate. Unfulfilled aspiration may always trouble him. But he will not be tormented in the same way as the man who, desiring to reach Mecca, and harried by the desire to reach Mecca, never leaves Brixton.

It is something to have left Brixton. Most of us have not left Brixton. We have not even taken a cab to Ludgate Circus and inquired from Cook's the price of a conducted tour. And our excuse to ourselves is that there are only twenty-four hours in the day.

If we further analyse our vague, uneasy aspiration, we shall, I think, see that it springs from a fixed idea that we ought to do something in addition to those things which we are loyally and morally obliged to do. We are obliged, by various codes written and unwritten, to maintain ourselves and our families (if any) in health and comfort, to pay our debts, to save, to increase our prosperity by increasing our efficiency. A task sufficiently difficult! A task which very few of us achieve! A task often beyond our skill! Yet, if we succeed in it, as we sometimes do, we are not satisfied; the skeleton is still with us.

And even when we realise that the task is beyond our skill, that our powers cannot cope with it, we feel that we should be less discontented if we gave to our powers, already overtaxed, something still further to do.

And such is, indeed, the fact. The wish to accomplish something outside their formal programme is common to all men who in the course of evolution have risen past a certain level.

Until an effort is made to satisfy that wish, the sense of uneasy waiting for something to start which has not started will remain to disturb the peace of the soul.

"A master in the art of living draws no sharp distinction between his work and his play; his labor and his leisure; his mind and his body; his education and his recreation. He hardly knows which is which. He simply pursues his vision of excellence through whatever he is doing, and leaves others to determine whether he is working or playing. To himself, he always appears to be doing both." —L.P. Jacks

Reveille
FROM *A SHROPSHIRE LAD*, 1896
By A.E. Houseman

Wake: the silver dusk returning
Up the beach of darkness brims,
And the ship of sunrise burning
Strands upon the eastern rims.

Wake: the vaulted shadow shatters,
Trampled to the floor it spanned,
And the tent of night in tatters
Straws the sky-pavilioned land.

Up, lad, up, 'tis late for lying:
Hear the drums of morning play;
Hark, the empty highways crying
"Who'll beyond the hills away?"

Towns and countries woo together,
Forelands beacon, belfries call;
Never lad that trod on leather
Lived to feast his heart with all.
Up, lad: thews that lie and cumber
Sunlit pallets never thrive;
Morns abed and daylight slumber
Were not meant for man alive.

Clay lies still, but blood's a rover;
Breath's a ware that will not keep.
Up, lad: when the journey's over
There'll be time enough to sleep.

"It is not necessary for a man to be actively bad in order to make a failure in life; simple inaction will accomplish it. Nature has everywhere written her protest against idleness; everything which ceases to struggle, which remains inactive, rapidly deteriorates. It is the struggle toward an ideal, the constant effort to get higher and further, which develops manhood and character." —James Terry White

Energetic Men
FROM *READINGS FOR YOUNG MEN, MERCHANTS, AND MEN OF BUSINESS*, 1859

We love upright, energetic men. Pull them this way, and then that way, and the other, and they only bend, but never break. Trip them down, and in a trice they are on their feet. Bury them in the mud, and in an hour they will be out and bright. They are not ever yawning away existence, or walking about the world as if they had come into it with only half their soul; you cannot keep them down; you cannot destroy them. But for these the world would soon degenerate. They are the salt of the earth. Who but they start any noble project? They build our cities and rear our manufactories; they whiten the ocean with their sails; they draw treasures from the mine; they plow the earth. Blessings on them! Look to them, young men, and take courage; imitate their example; catch the spirit of their energy and enterprise, and you will deserve, and no doubt command, success.

> *"Rest not! Life is sweeping by,*
> *Go and dare, before you die;*
> *Something mighty and sublime*
> *Leave behind to conquer time!"*
> —*Johann Wolfgang von Goethe*

The Improvement of Spare Moments

FROM *PUSHING TO THE FRONT*, 1894
By Orison Swett Marden

On the floor of the gold-working room, in the United States Mint at Philadelphia, there is a wooden lattice-work which is taken up when the floor is swept, and the fine particles of gold-dust, thousands of dollars' yearly, are thus saved. So every successful man has a kind of network to catch "the raspings and parings of existence, those leavings of days and wee bits of hours" which most people sweep into the waste of life. He who hoards and turns to account all odd minutes, half hours, unexpected holidays, gaps between times, and chasms of waiting for unpunctual persons, achieves results which astonish those who have not mastered this most valuable secret.

The days come to us like friends in disguise, bringing priceless gifts from an unseen hand; but, if we do not use them, they are borne silently away, never to return. Each successive morning new gifts are brought, but if we failed to accept those that were brought yesterday and the day before, we become less and less able to turn them to account, until the ability to appreciate and utilize them is exhausted. Wisely was it said that lost wealth may be regained by industry and economy, lost knowledge by study, lost health by temperance and medicine, but lost time is gone forever.

"Oh, it's only five minutes or ten minutes till meal-time; there's no time to do anything now," is one of the commonest expressions heard in the family. But what monuments have been built up by poor boys with no chance, out of broken fragments of time which many of us throw away! The very hours you have wasted, if improved, might have insured your success.

The author of "Paradise Lost" was a teacher, Secretary of the Commonwealth, Secretary of the Lord Protector, and had to write his sublime poetry whenever he could snatch a few minutes from a busy life. John Stuart Mill did much of his best work as a writer while a clerk in the East India House. Galileo was a surgeon, yet to the improvement of his spare moments the world owes some of its greatest discoveries.

If a genius like Gladstone carried through life a little book in his pocket lest an unexpected spare moment slip from his grasp, what should we of common abilities not resort to, to save the precious moments from oblivion? … Many a great man has snatched his reputation from odd bits of time which others, who wonder at their failure to get on, throw away. In Dante's time nearly every literary man in Italy was a hardworking merchant, physician, statesman, judge, or soldier.

Oh, the power of ceaseless industry to perform miracles!

One hour a day withdrawn from frivolous pursuits and profitably employed would enable any man of ordinary capacity to master a complete science. One hour a day would in ten years make an ignorant man a well-informed man. … In an hour a day a boy or a girl could read twenty pages thoughtfully—over seven thousand pages, or eighteen large volumes in a year.

An hour a day might make all the difference between bare existence and useful, happy living. An hour a day might make—nay, has made—an unknown man a famous one, a useless man a benefactor to his race. Consider, then, the mighty possibilities of two—four—yes, six hours a day that are, on the average, thrown away by young men.

Every young man should have a hobby to occupy his leisure hours, something useful to which he can turn with delight. It might be in line with his work or otherwise, only *his heart must be in it.*

If one chooses wisely, the study, research, and occupation that a hobby confers will broaden character and transform the home.

"He has nothing to prevent him but too much idleness, which, I have observed," says Burke, "fills up a man's time much more completely and leaves him less his own master, than any sort of employment whatsoever."

Some boys will pick up a good education in the odds and ends of time which others carelessly throw away, as one man saves a fortune by small economies which others disdain to practise. What young man is too busy to get an hour a day for self-improvement?

Great men have ever been misers of moments. Cicero said: "What others give to public shows and entertainments, nay, even to mental and bodily rest, I give to the study of philosophy." Lord Bacon's fame springs from the work of his leisure hours while Chancellor of England. During an interview with a great monarch, Goethe suddenly excused himself, went into an adjoining room and wrote down a thought for his "Faust," lest it should be forgotten. ... Pope would often rise in the night to write out thoughts that would not come during the busy day. Grote wrote his matchless "History of Greece" during the hours of leisure snatched from his duties as a banker.

Dr. Darwin composed most of his works by writing his thoughts on scraps of paper wherever he happened to be. Watt learned chemistry and mathematics while working at his trade of a mathematical instrument-maker. Henry Kirke White learned Greek while walking to and from the lawyer's office where he was studying. Dr. Burney learned Italian and French on horseback. Matthew Hale wrote his "Contemplations" while traveling on his circuit as judge.

The present time is the raw material out of which we make whatever we will. Do not brood over the past, or dream of the future, but seize the instant and *get your lesson from the hour*. The man is yet unborn who rightly measures and fully realizes the value of an hour. As Fenelon says, God never gives but one moment at a time, and does not give a second until he withdraws the first.

The worst of a lost hour is not so much in the wasted time as in the wasted power. Idleness rusts the nerves and makes the muscles creak. Work has system, laziness has none.

In factories for making cloth a single broken thread ruins a whole web; it is traced back to the girl who made the blunder and the loss is deducted from her wages. But who shall pay for the broken threads in life's great web? We cannot throw back and forth an empty shuttle; threads of some kind follow every movement as we weave the web of our fate. It may be a shoddy thread of wasted hours or lost opportunities that will mar the fabric and mortify the workman forever; or it may be a golden thread which will add to its beauty and luster.

"Opportunity is missed by most people because it is dressed in overalls and looks like work." —Thomas Edison

Opportunity
By Edward Rowland Sill, 1880

This I beheld, or dreamed it in a dream:—
There spread a cloud of dust along a plain;
And underneath the cloud, or in it, raged
A furious battle, and men yelled, and swords
Shocked upon swords and shields. A prince's banner
Wavered, then staggered backward, hemmed by foes.
A craven hung along the battle's edge,
And thought: "Had I a sword of keener steel—
That blue blade that the king's son bears—but this
Blunt thing—!" he snapt and flung it from his hand,
And lowering crept away and left the field.
Then came the king's son, wounded, sore bestead,
And weaponless, and saw the broken sword,
Hilt-buried in the dry and trodden sand,
And ran and snatched it, and with battle-shout
Lifted afresh he hewed his enemy down,
And saved a great cause on that heroic day.

"Mankind is more indebted to industry than ingenuity; the gods set up their favors at a price, and industry is the purchaser." —Joseph Addison

Dead Work

FROM *SELF-CULTURE THROUGH THE VOCATION*, 1914
By Edward Howard Griggs

There is an almost universal optical illusion with reference to work: each of us is fully conscious of the dead work in his own calling, because he must fulfill it; with the tasks of others, he sees only the finished product. Thus each is inclined to exaggerate the dead work in his own vocation and to envy the apparently easier and happier tasks of others. You sit down in an audience room, and some master at the piano sweeps you out on to the bosom of the sea of emotion, playing with you at his will. The evening of melody is over; there is the moment of awed silence and then the storm of applause; you go home exclaiming, "What genius!" O yes, it is genius: someone has defined genius as the capacity for hard work. Genius is more than that—much more; but no exaggerated talent would take a man far, without the capacity for hard work; and what you forget, as you listen to the finished art of the master genius, is the days and nights of consecrated toil, foregoing, not only dissipation, but even innocent pleasures others take as their natural right, that the artist might master and keep the mastery of the technique of his art.

It is said of Euclid, formulator of the earliest of the sciences, geometry, that on one occasion he was called in to teach a certain king of Egypt his new science. He began as we begin, with definition, axiom and proposition—we have not improved appreciably upon his text-book; and the king grew restless and indignant: "Must a Pharaoh learn like a common slave?" Euclid, with that pride in knowing one thing well, that everyone ought to have who knows one science thoroughly to the end, responded: "There is no royal road to geometry!" We can universalize the statement: there is no royal road to anything on earth—perhaps in heaven either—worth having, except the one broad, open highway, with no toll-gates upon it, of dead, hard, consistent work through the days and years. Spinoza said—it is the last word in his *Ethic*: "All noble things are as difficult as they are rare;" and we may add, they are rare because they are difficult.

> *"Be regular and orderly in your daily affairs that you may be violent and original in your work." —Gustave Flaubert*

The Daily Schedules of
Theodore Roosevelt and Benjamin Franklin

In the introduction to this chapter, we detailed how much two great men from history, Benjamin Franklin and Theodore Roosevelt, accomplished during their lives. One of the secrets to their inspiring success was the way in which they effectively utilized their time each day. For a closer examination of just how they did this, here is a look at each man's daily schedule.

BENJAMIN FRANKLIN'S DAILY SCHEDULE

Seeking to attain "moral perfection," Benjamin Franklin established a program in which he strove to live thirteen different virtues. As he particularly struggled with the "precept of Order," he kept the following schedule inside the little notebook in which he kept track of his adherence to the virtues.

SCHEME.

Hours.

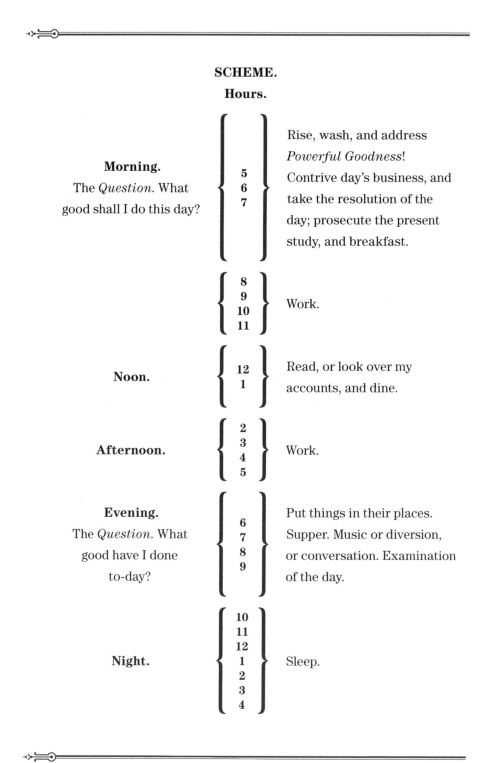

Morning. The *Question*. What good shall I do this day?	5 6 7	Rise, wash, and address *Powerful Goodness*! Contrive day's business, and take the resolution of the day; prosecute the present study, and breakfast.
	8 9 10 11	Work.
Noon.	12 1	Read, or look over my accounts, and dine.
Afternoon.	2 3 4 5	Work.
Evening. The *Question*. What good have I done to-day?	6 7 8 9	Put things in their places. Supper. Music or diversion, or conversation. Examination of the day.
Night.	10 11 12 1 2 3 4	Sleep.

Theodore Roosevelt's Daily Schedule

When campaigning for the vice presidency in 1900, TR spent eight weeks barnstorming around the country. Traveling by train, he covered 21,000 miles visiting twenty-four states. All along the way he made speeches, delivering 700 in all to 3 million people.

His daily schedule during this time was recorded by a man who accompanied him on the tour.

7:00 A.M.—Breakfast.

7:30 A.M.—A speech.

8:00 A.M.—Reading a historical work.

9:00 A.M.—A speech.

10:00 A.M.—Dictating letters.

11:00 A.M.—Discussing Montana mines.

11:30 A.M.—A speech.

12:00 P.M.—Reading an ornithological work.

12:30 P.M.—A speech.

1:00 P.M.—Lunch.

1:30 P.M.—A speech.

2:30 P.M.—Reading Sir Walter Scott.

3:00 P.M.—Answering telegrams.

3:45 P.M.—A speech.

4:00 P.M.—Meeting the press.

4:30 P.M.—Reading.

5:00 P.M.—A speech.

6:00 P.M.—Reading.

7:00 P.M.—Supper.

8:00 to 10:00 P.M.—Speaking.

11:00 P.M.—Reading alone in his car.

12:00 P.M.—To bed.

Theodore Roosevelt's System of Energizing
FROM "THE POWERS OF A STRENUOUS PRESIDENT," 1908
By "K"

The following excerpt from an article in *The American Magazine* illuminates the way in which Roosevelt's energy and discipline made this kind of extraordinary productivity possible.

The President is the very incarnation of order and regularity in his work. That is part of his system of energizing. Every morning Secretary Loeb places a typewritten list of his engagements for the day on his desk, sometimes reduced to five-minute intervals. And no railroad engineer runs more sharply upon his schedule than he. His watch comes out of his pocket, he cuts off an interview, or signs a paper, and turns instantly, according to his time-table, to the next engagement. If there is an interval anywhere left over he chinks in the time by reading a paragraph of history from the book that lies always ready at his elbow or by writing two or three sentences in an article on Irish folk-lore, or bear-hunting.

Thus he never stops running, even while he stokes and fires; the throttle is always open; the engine is always under a full head of steam. I have seen schedules of his engagements which showed that he was constantly occupied from nine o'clock in the morning, when he takes his regular walk in the White House Park with Mrs. Roosevelt, until midnight, with guests at both luncheon and dinner. And when he goes to bed he is able to disabuse his mind instantly of every care and worry and go straight to sleep, and he sleeps with perfect normality and on schedule time.

I have been thinking back over Roosevelt's career in the White House and I cannot now remember to have heard that he was ever ill or even indisposed as other men sometimes are. Like any good engineer, he keeps his machinery in such excellent condition that he never has a breakdown.

Thus we have the spectacle of a man of ordinary abilities who has succeeded through the simple device of self-control and self-discipline, of using every power he possesses to its utmost limit.

"Let us realize that the privilege to work is a gift, that power to work is a blessing, that love of work is success." —David O. McKay

The Farmer and His Sons
An Aesop's Fable

A Farmer being on the point of death, and wishing to show his sons the way to success in farming, called them to him, and said, "My children, I am now departing from this life, but all that I have to leave you, you will find in the vineyard." The sons, supposing that he referred to some hidden treasure, as soon as the old man was dead, set to work with their spades and ploughs and every implement that was at hand, and turned up the soil over and over again. They found indeed no treasure; but the vines, strengthened and improved by this thorough tillage, yielded a finer vintage than they had ever yielded before, and more than repaid the young husbandmen for all their trouble.

Industry is in itself a treasure.

"It is better to wear out than to rust out." —Bishop Richard Cumberland

Now
FROM *READINGS FOR YOUNG MEN, MERCHANTS, AND MEN OF BUSINESS*, 1859

"Now" is the constant syllable ticking from the clock of Time. "Now" is the watchword of the wise. "Now" is on the banner of the prudent. Let us keep this little word always in our mind; and, whenever any thing presents itself to us in the shape of work, whether mental or physical, we should do it with all our might, remembering that "now" is the only time for us. It is indeed a sorry way to get through the world by putting off till to-morrow, saying, "then" I will do it. No! This will never answer. "Now" is ours; "Then" may never be.

"Industry is the enemy of melancholy." —William F. Buckley Jr.

We Do Not Labor That We May Be Idle

FROM *NICOMACHEAN ETHICS*, C. 350 B.C.

By Aristotle

We do not labor that we may be idle; but, as Anarchis justly said, we are idle that we may labor with more effect; that is, we have recourse to sports and amusements as refreshing cordials after contentious exertions, that, having reposed in such diversions for a while, we may recommence our labors with increased vigor. The weakness of human nature requires frequent remissions of energy; but these rests and pauses are only the better to prepare us for enjoying the pleasures of activity. The amusements of life, therefore, are but preludes to its business, the place of which they cannot possibly supply; and its happiness, because its business, consists in the exercise of those virtuous energies which constitute the worth and dignity of our nature. Inferior pleasures may be enjoyed by the fool and the slave as completely as by the hero or the sage. But who will ascribe the happiness of a man to him, who by his character and condition, is disqualified for manly pursuits?

The Village Blacksmith

FROM *BALLADS AND OTHER POEMS*, 1841
By Henry Wadsworth Longfellow

Under a spreading chestnut tree
The village smithy stands;
The smith, a mighty man is he,
With large and sinewy hands;
And the muscles of his brawny arms
Are strong as iron bands.

His hair is crisp, and black, and long,
His face is like the tan;
His brow is wet with honest sweat,
He earns whate'er he can,
And looks the whole world in the face,
For he owes not any man.

Week in, week out, from morn till night,
You can hear his bellows blow;
You can hear him swing his heavy sledge,
With measured beat and slow,
Like a sexton ringing the village bell,
When the evening sun is low.
And children coming home from school
Look in at the open door;
They love to see the flaming forge,
And hear the bellows roar,
And catch the burning sparks that fly
Like chaff from a threshing floor.

He goes on Sunday to the church,
And sits among his boys;

He hears the parson pray and preach,
He hears his daughter's voice,
Singing in the village choir,
And it makes his heart rejoice.

It sounds to him like her mother's voice,
Singing in Paradise!
He needs must think of her once more,
How in the grave she lies;
And with his hard, rough hand he wipes
A tear out of his eyes.

Toiling,—rejoicing,—sorrowing,
Onwards through life he goes;
Each morning sees some task begin,
Each evening sees it close;
Something attempted, something done,
Has earned a night's repose.
Thanks, thanks to thee, my worthy friend,
For the lesson thou hast taught!
Thus at the flaming forge of life
Our fortunes must be wrought;
Thus on its sounding anvil shaped
Each burning deed and thought!

"It is not enough to be industrious; so are the ants. What are you industrious about?" —Henry David Thoreau

Having an Aim

FROM *TRAITS OF CHARACTER*, 1898
By Henry F. Kletzing

A light snow had fallen and a company of schoolboys wished to make the most of it. It was too dry for snowballing. It was proposed that a number of boys walk across a meadow near by and see who could make the straightest track. On examination it was found that only one could be called straight. When asked, two of them said they went as straight as they could without looking at anything but the ground. The third said, "I fixed my eye on that tree on yonder hill and never looked away till I reached the fence."

We often miss the end of life by having no object before us.

In one of his fiercest battles, it is known that Philip, King of Macedon, lost his eye from a bowshot. And when the soldiers picked up the shaft which wounded him, they perceived upon it these words: "To Philip's eye!" The archer was so certain of his skill that he had announced his aim beforehand. It is a pitiable mistake, when one comes to care, like a lawn

CHAPTER THREE

sportsman, more for a stately posture and a graceful attitude than for the mark he aims at.

Once when the British Science Association met in Dublin, Mr. Huxley arrived late at the city. Fearing to miss the president's address he hurried from the train, jumped into a jaunting-car and breathlessly said to the driver, "Drive fast, I am in a hurry!" The driver slashed his horse with his whip and went spinning down the street. Suddenly it occurred to Mr. Huxley that he had probably not instructed the driver properly. He shouted to the driver, "Do you know where I want to go?" "No, yer 'onor," was Pat's laughing reply, "but I'm driving fast all the while." There are many people who go through the world in this way. They are always going, and sometimes at great speed, but never get anywhere. They have no definite purpose and never accomplish anything.

It is the man that has an aim that accomplishes something in this world. A young man fired with a determined purpose to win in a particular aim has fought half the battle. What was it that has made men great in the past? One dominant aim! Names of great men at once suggest their life purpose. No one thinks of a Watt aside from the steam engine, a Howe suggests the sewing machine, a Bell the telephone, an Edison the electric light, a Morse the telegraph, a Cyrus Field the Atlantic cable. A man of one talent, fixed on a definite object, accomplishes more than a man of ten talents who spreads himself over a large surface. To keep your gun from scattering, put in a single shot.

"The idle pass through life leaving as little trace of their existence as foam upon the water or smoke upon the air; whereas the industrious stamp their character upon their age, and influence not only their own but all succeeding generations."
—*Samuel Smiles*

The Strenuous Life

FROM *THE STRENUOUS LIFE: ESSAYS AND ADDRESSES*, 1902
By Theodore Roosevelt

I wish to preach, not the doctrine of ignoble ease, but the doctrine of the strenuous life, the life of toil and effort, of labor and strife; to preach that highest form of success which comes, not to the man who desires mere easy peace, but to the man who does not shrink from danger, from hardship, or from bitter toil, and who out of these wins the splendid ultimate triumph.

A life of slothful ease, a life of that peace which springs merely from lack either of desire or of power to strive after great things, is as little worthy of a nation as of an individual. I ask only that what every self-respecting American demands from himself and from his sons shall be demanded of the American nation as a whole. Who among you would teach your boys that ease, that peace, is to be the first consideration in their eyes—to be the ultimate goal after which they strive? You men of Chicago have made this city great, you men of Illinois have done your share, and more than your share, in making America great, because you neither preach nor practise such a doctrine. You work yourselves, and you bring up your sons to work. If you are rich and are worth your salt, you will teach your sons that though they may have leisure, it is not to be spent in idleness; for wisely used leisure merely means that those who possess it, being free from the necessity of working for their livelihood, are all the more bound to carry on some kind of non-remunerative work in science, in letters, in art, in exploration, in historical research—work of the type we most need in this country, the successful carrying out of which reflects most honor upon the nation. We do not admire the man of timid peace. We admire the man who embodies victorious effort; the man who never wrongs his neighbor, who is prompt to help a friend, but who has those virile qualities necessary to win in the stern strife of actual life. It is hard to fail, but it is worse never to have tried to succeed. In this life we get nothing save by effort.

Opportunity

By John James Ingalls

....

Written by John James Ingalls (1833–1900), a U.S. Senator from Kansas, this poem was said to be Theodore Roosevelt's favorite; when he was president, an autographed copy of the poem was the only thing besides a portrait to hang in his executive office in the White House.

....

Master of human destinies am I;
Fame, love, and fortune on my footsteps wait.
Cities and fields I walk; I penetrate
Deserts and seas remote, and passing by
Hovel and mart and palace—soon or late
I knock unbidden once at every gate!
If sleeping, wake—if feasting, rise before
I turn away. It is the hour of fate,
And they who follow me reach every state
Mortals desire, and conquer every foe
Save death; but those who doubt or hesitate
Condemned to failure, penury, and woe,
Seek me in vain, and uselessly implore.
I answer not, and I return no more!

"Industry, thrift and self-control are not sought because they create wealth, but because they create character."
—Calvin Coolidge

What Man Understands That He Is Dying Daily?

FROM *MORAL LETTERS TO LUCILIUS*, 65 A.D.

By Seneca

The Roman Stoic philosopher Seneca wrote letters to his friend Lucilius in which he espoused the tenets of a life aligned with Stoic ideals. These letters were compiled in Epistulae morales ad Lucilium (Moral Letters to Lucilius). In this letter, Seneca beseeches Lucilius to use his time wisely.

Continue to act thus, my dear Lucilius—set yourself free for your own sake; gather and save your time, which 'til lately has been forced from you, or filched away, or has merely slipped from your hands. Make yourself believe the truth of my words—that certain moments are torn from us, that some are gently removed, and that others glide beyond our reach. The most disgraceful kind of loss, however, is that due to carelessness. Furthermore, if you will pay close heed to the problem, you will find that the largest portion of our life passes while we are doing ill, a goodly share while we are doing nothing, and the whole while we are doing that which is not to the purpose. What man can you show me who places any value on his time, who reckons the worth of each day, who understands that he is dying daily? For we are mistaken when we look forward to death; the major portion of death has already passed. Whatever years be behind us are in death's hands.

Therefore, Lucilius, do as you write me that you are doing: hold every hour in your grasp. Lay hold of to-day's task, and you will not need to depend so much upon to-morrow's. While we are postponing, life speeds by. Nothing, Lucilius, is ours, except time. We were entrusted by nature with the ownership of this single thing, so fleeting and slippery that anyone who will can oust us from possession. What fools these mortals be! They allow the cheapest and most useless things, which can easily be replaced, to be charged in the reckoning, after they have acquired them; but they never regard themselves as in debt when they have received some of that precious commodity—time! And yet time is the one loan which even a grateful recipient cannot repay.

"Nihil sine labor." ("Nothing without labor.")
—*Latin maxim*

Ben Franklin's Maxims on Industry

Early to bed and early to rise, makes a man healthy, wealthy and wise.

Diligence is the mother of good luck.

God helps them that help themselves.

At the working man's house hunger looks in, but dares not enter.

For industry pays debts, while despair increaseth them.

By diligence and patience the mouse ate in two the cable.

Little strokes fell great oaks.

Since thou art not sure of a minute, throw not away an hour.

Trouble springs from idleness, and grievous toil from needless ease.

Many, without labor, would live by their wits only, but they break for want of stock.

Sloth makes all things difficult, but industry all things easy.

Dost thou love life? Then do not squander time, for that is the stuff life is made of.

Sloth, like rust, consumes faster than labor wears, while the used key is always bright.

There will be sleeping enough in the grave.

Lost time is never found again.

Laziness travels so slowly, that Poverty soon overtakes him.

Industry need not wish, and he that lives upon hopes will die fasting.

Plough deep, while sluggards sleep.

Handle your tools without mittens; the cat in gloves catches no mice.

Constant dropping wears away stones.

A ploughman on his legs is higher than a gentleman on his knees.

"The chiefest action for a man of great spirit is never to be out of action ... the soul was never put into the body to stand still." —John Webster

The Choice of Hercules

FROM *THE MEMORABILIA*
By Xenophon, c. 371 B.C.

· ·

Xenophon (430–354 B.C.) was an ancient Greek historian and student of the philosopher Socrates. His *Memorabilia* is a collection of Socratic dialogues which purports to record the defense Socrates made for himself during his trial before the Athenians. While arguing against indolence and for the beneficial effects of labor, Socrates cites a story told by the Sophist Prodicus: The Choice of Hercules.

This story was popular throughout the eighteenth century; John Adams used it to guide his life and wished to make an illustration of the tale the design for the Great Seal of the new nation. It is a fable used to convey a profound truth: that there can be no sweet without the bitter, no growth and no true happiness without work.

· ·

When Hercules was in that part of his youth in which it was natural for him to consider what course of life he ought to pursue, he one day retired into a desert, where the silence and solitude of the place very much favored his meditations.

As he was musing on his present condition, and very much perplexed in himself, on the state of life he should choose, he saw two women of a larger stature than ordinary, approaching towards him. One of them had a very noble air, and graceful deportment; her beauty was natural and easy, her person clean and unspotted … her motions and behavior full of modesty, and her raiment was white as snow. The other wanted all the native beauty and proportion of the former; her person was swelled, by luxury and ease, to a size quite disproportioned and uncomely. She had painted her complexion, that it might seem fairer and more ruddy than it really was, and endeavored to appear more graceful than ordinary in her bearing, by a mixture of affectation in all her gestures. She cast her eyes frequently upon herself, then turned them on those that were present, to see whether any one regarded her, and now and then looked on the figure she made in her own shadow.

As they drew nearer, the former continued the same composed pace, while the latter, striving to get before her, ran up to Hercules, and addressed herself to him:

"My dear Hercules," says she, "I find you are very much divided in your thoughts, upon the way of life that you ought to choose; be my friend, and follow me; I will lead you into the possession of pleasure, and out of the reach of pain, and remove you from all the noise and disquietude of business. The affairs of either peace or war, shall have no power to disturb you. Your whole employment shall be to make your life easy, and to entertain every sense with its proper gratifications. Sumptuous tables, beds of roses, clouds of perfumes, concerts of music, crowds of beauties, are all in readiness to receive you. Come along with me into this region of delights, this world of pleasure, and bid farewell forever, to care, to pain, to business."

Hercules, hearing the lady talk after this manner, desired to know her name; to which she answered, "My friends, and those who are well acquainted with me, call me Happiness; but my enemies, and those who would injure my reputation, have given me the name of Pleasure."

By this time the other lady came up, who addressed herself to the young hero in a very different manner.

"Hercules," says she, "I offer myself to you, because I know you are descended from the gods, and give proofs of that descent by your love to virtue, and application to the studies proper for your age. This makes me hope you will gain, both for yourself and me, an immortal reputation. But, before I invite you into my society and friendship, I will be open and sincere with you, and must lay down this, as an established truth, that there is nothing truly valuable which can be purchased without pains and labor. The gods have set a price upon every real and noble pleasure. If you would gain the favor of the Deity, you must be at the pains of worshiping him: if the friendship of good men, you must study to oblige them: if you would be honored by your country, you must take care to serve it. In short, if you would be eminent in war or peace, you must become master of all the qualifications that can make you so. These are the only terms and conditions upon which I can propose happiness."

The goddess of Pleasure here broke in upon her discourse: "You see," said she, "Hercules, by her own confession, the way to her pleasures is long and difficult; whereas, that which I propose is short and easy." "Alas!" said the other lady, whose visage glowed with passion, made up of scorn and pity, "What are the pleasures you propose? To eat before you are hungry, drink before you are athirst, sleep before you are tired; to gratify your appetites before they are raised. You never heard the most delicious music, which is the praise of one's own self; nor saw the most beautiful object, which is the work of one's own hands. Your votaries pass away their youth in a dream of mistaken pleasures, while they are hoarding up anguish, torment, and remorse, for old age."

"As for me, I am the friend of gods and of good men, an agreeable companion to the artisan, a household guardian to the fathers of families, a patron and protector of servants, an associate in all true and generous friendships. The banquets of my votaries are never costly, but always delicious; for none eat and drink at them, who are not invited by hunger and thirst. Their slumbers are sound, and their wakings cheerful. My young men have the pleasure of hearing themselves praised by those who are in years; and those who are in years, of being honored by those who are young. In a word, my followers are favored by the gods, beloved by their acquaintance, esteemed by their country, and after the close of their labors, honored by posterity."

INDUSTRY

CHAPTER FOUR
RESOLUTION

If industry is the motor that propels men to greatness, then resolution is the gasoline that fuels the engine. History is full of men who displayed bursts of energetic genius, but weren't able to feed and sustain their initial fire. Men who *tried* but who did not *persevere*. Their flames went out as quickly as they ignited.

Resolution is a defining characteristic of the mature masculine. A boy will dabble in many things, but will seldom finish what he starts. When a challenge arises or when he grows bored with a project, he'll move on to something else. So too the irresolute man. In place of dusty toys, he leaves behind the fixer-upper car on cinder blocks in the driveway, the half-finished deck out back, the angry first wife, the reams of paper waiting to become the Great American Novel.

It is easy to make a choice, much harder to endure in that decision and see it through to the very end. Starting a new job or project is fun and exciting. The feeling of new romance or adventure, of changing one's life and turning over a new leaf, leaves a man flush with a boyish enthusiasm that will carry him through the first few weeks or months of an endeavor. But many men throw in the towel when the "honeymoon period" ends, when challenges arise, and the toil becomes tough. Then it's on to the next thing. The irresolute man goes from one thing to another, ever in search of the illusory pursuit that will remain as easy and enjoyable in the middle as it was at the beginning.

A mature man, on the other hand, is able to power through the doldrums and the setbacks that beset him. When the initial passion fades, he is able to switch to another fuel source, that of willpower and commitment. He understands that enduring greatness comes to the man whose resolve remains unshaken through both thick and thin. The resolute man begins with the end in mind and finishes what he starts, no matter what. He is willing to endure suffering and hardship for glory and honor.

Resolution involves a combination of hardihood, perseverance, and decisiveness, and this chapter explores each of these important dimensions of the virtue. The selections are designed to fill the tank of your resolve, giving fuel to your drive and determination.

"The longer I live, the more I am certain that the great difference between men—between the feeble and the powerful, the great and the insignificant—is energy, invincible determination—a purpose once fixed, and then—death or victory! That quality will do anything that can be done in this world, and no talents, no circumstances, no opportunities, will make a two-legged creature a man without it." —Sir Thomas Fowell Buxton

Perseverance: A Double Vitality

FROM *READINGS FOR YOUNG MEN, MERCHANTS, AND MEN OF BUSINESS*, 1859

[Perseverance] means the steady pursuit of a plan, whether good or bad; but it would be very unwise to persevere in a plan which conscience or practice had proved to be bad. In actual life, where there are so many different pursuits, and different ways of doing the same thing, it means steadiness in the execution of whatever plan is determined upon.

An accomplished American says, "That the man who is perpetually hesitating which of two things he will do first, will do neither. The man who resolves, but suffers his resolution to be changed by the first counter-suggestion of a friend—who fluctuates from opinion to opinion, from plan to plan, and veers like a weathercock to every point of the compass with every breath of caprice that blows—can never accomplish any thing great or useful. Instead of being progressive in any thing he will be at best stationary, and, more probably, retrograde in all. It is only the man who carries into his pursuits that great quality which Lucan ascribes to Caesar, *Nescia virtus stare loco* [his energy could never rest]—who first consults wisely, then resolves firmly, and then executes his purpose with inflexible perseverance, undismayed by those petty difficulties which daunt a weaker spirit—that can advance to eminence in any line."

If any one is in doubt as to what perseverance is, he may soon find out by a little observation. Look round among your friends and acquaintances; there is perhaps among them an example of perseverance. Keep your eye on him for a time; does it not seem as though he had a double vitality within him, some other man's life as well as his own? It is true that his heart beats and his blood circulates in the same way as that of other men, but you cannot help fancying that there is something else in the circulation invigorating every nerve and muscle, only to cease when the wonderful machine stands still. If at times it seems to be idle, you may be sure that it is not real idleness—but only a pause for a new start.

The question is sometimes asked, whether a man may learn to be per-severing—for if perseverance be of such value and benefit, why should not all possess it? The answer is, that a man may learn to persevere if he will. To do this, he must begin by believing that he can do it. He must not be disheartened at the outset by certain stock phrases which seem to tell against him, such a "prerogative of genius," or "predominance of the natal star;" he must set these down as "cabalistic nonsense," and confide in the assurance that "diligence overcomes all." Truly has it been said, that "there are few difficulties that hold out against real attacks; they fly, like the visible horizon, before those who advance. A passionate desire and unwearied will can perform impossibilities, or what seem to be such to the cold and feeble. If we do but go on, some unseen path will open upon the hills. Nothing good or great is to be attained without courage and industry. Resist unto the end. ... Let no one doubt that perseverance may be learned until he has tried bravely and honestly for a year.

To those who can and do persevere, we would say: Go on; but see that what you strive for is worth the effort. Remember that there is a false as well as a true perseverance, and it is possible to waste the energies of a life on unworthy objects. "By their fruits shall ye know them." We are commanded to be "diligent in business," but this is not the whole. We must persevere with our inward life as well as our outward life; there should be harmony between the two, if we are to feel that each day, as it passes, has helped to refine our mind, soften our heart, or heighten our love of justice.

To those who persevere only by fits and starts—now hot, now cold— we would say, "Never give up." Do not lose courage or grow weary. Slow as the tortoise crept, he reached the goal before the sleeping hare. If you cannot run, walk; if you cannot fly, plod. Plodding, humble as it seems, has done wonders, and will do more yet. Consider, furthermore, that when the reward comes, it is scarcely ever such as we had anticipated. We may have aimed at getting rich; the riches do not come. But, instead thereof, we find ourselves rich in mind; conscious of having striven manfully to do the duty that lay before us, and in so doing have armed ourselves with a reliant spirit, which passes by small trials, and looks on great ones with calm courage. View it as we will, the conclusion is inevitable, that perseverance is its own reward.

Winston Churchill's Speeches During the Fall of France

On May 10, 1940, Germany invaded Belgium, the Netherlands, and France. On the same day, the Prime Minister of Britain, Neville Chamberlain, resigned and was replaced by Winston Churchill. On the 13th, Churchill made his first appearance before the House of Commons as the Head of Her Majesty's Government.

Despite receiving a tepid reception from that body, he issued a masterful call-to-arms, offering unshakeable resolve to a country frightened that it would be next to fall to German forces.

••

May 13, 1940

I would say to the House, as I said to those who have joined the government: "I have nothing to offer but blood, toil, tears and sweat."

We have before us an ordeal of the most grievous kind. We have before us many, many long months of struggle and of suffering. You ask, what is our policy? I will say: It is to wage war, by sea, land and air, with all our might and with all the strength that God can give us; to wage war against a monstrous tyranny, never surpassed in the dark and lamentable catalogue of human crime. That is our policy. You ask, what is our aim? I can answer in one word: victory; victory at all costs, victory in spite of all terror, victory, however long and hard the road may be; for without victory, there is no survival. Let that be realized; no survival for the British Empire, no survival for all that the British Empire has stood for, no survival for the urge and impulse of the ages, that mankind will move forward towards its goal. But I take up my task with buoyancy and hope. I feel sure that our cause will not be suffered to fail among men. At this time I feel entitled to claim the aid of all, and I say, "Come then, let us go forward together with our united strength."

CHAPTER FOUR

After a devastating defeat in which British troops had to be evacuated from Dunkirk, France, Churchill once more sought to shore up his countrymen's resolve to continue fighting.

June 4, 1940

I have, myself, full confidence that if all do their duty, if nothing is neglected, and if the best arrangements are made, as they are being made, we shall prove ourselves once again able to defend our Island home, to ride out the storm of war, and to outlive the menace of tyranny, if necessary for years, if necessary alone. At any rate, that is what we are going to try to do. That is the resolve of His Majesty's Government—every man of them. That is the will of Parliament and the nation. The British Empire and the French Republic, linked together in their cause and in their need, will defend to the death their native soil, aiding each other like good comrades to the utmost of their strength. Even though large tracts of Europe and many old and famous States have fallen or may fall into the grip of the Gestapo and all the odious apparatus of Nazi rule, we shall not flag or fail. We shall go on to the end, we shall fight in France, we shall fight on the seas and oceans, we shall fight with growing confidence and growing strength in the air, we shall defend our Island, whatever the cost may be, we shall fight on the beaches, we shall fight on the landing grounds, we shall fight in the fields and in the streets, we shall fight in the hills; we shall never surrender.

"To think we are able is almost to be so; to determine upon attainment is frequently attainment itself. Thus earnest resolution has often seemed to have about it almost a savor of omnipotence." —Samuel Smiles

Invictus

FROM *A BOOK OF VERSES*, 1889
By William Ernest Henley

After contracting tuberculosis of the bone at age twelve, and having one leg amputated below the knee at age eighteen, doctors informed William Ernest Henley that they would have to amputate his other leg to save his life. Refusing to accept this diagnosis, the poet chose to be hospitalized for several years and endure numerous painful surgeries in order to save the leg. He penned this famous poem from his hospital bed, resolute in his determination to lead a full and vigorous life. That he did, eventually leaving the hospital with the leg intact and going on to become a successful and respected poet, critic, and literary editor.

Invictus, Latin for "unconquerable," has become the watchword of every man who looks life's challenges in the eye and refuses to blink.

Out of the night that covers me,
Black as the pit from pole to pole,
I thank whatever gods may be
For my unconquerable soul.

In the fell clutch of circumstance
I have not winced nor cried aloud.
Under the bludgeonings of chance
My head is bloody, but unbowed.

Beyond this place of wrath and tears
Looms but the Horror of the shade,
And yet the menace of the years
Finds and shall find me unafraid.

It matters not how strait the gate,
How charged with punishments the scroll,
I am the master of my fate:
I am the captain of my soul.

Self-Measuring Questions
Concerning the Characteristic of Hardihood

FROM *HOW TO CHOOSE THE RIGHT VOCATION*, 1917
By Holmes Whittier Merton

••

Hardihood is a manly trait that encompasses the boldness, confidence, and daring to attempt difficult and risky feats, as well as the grit and resiliency to keep going when faced with setbacks and criticism. These questions are designed to help you evaluate your personal level of hardihood.

••

Have I "stout and persistent courage" or am I only courageous under excitement or stimulation of some kind?

Do I have to screw up my courage to meet difficult situations?

Am I conscious of being mentally and physically rugged?

Do I challenge hardships or do I try to avoid hardships and difficulties by following "the line of least resistance?"

Do I hesitate about trying out my powers in unused directions that demand fortitude or courage?

Have I the courage to blaze new lines of action when success seems reasonably certain or do I wait until others have occupied the "strategic positions?"

Does the element of personal risk in sports, travel, adventures or vocations count greatly with me?

Does that which is unknown or untried affright or allure me?

Am I attracted or repelled by the hazardousness of life-saving callings?

Am I resolute and clear-headed in the presence of imminent danger or do I quail or become panic-stricken?

As boy or man, have I ever shown *individual* heroism or is my bravery always of the mass or mob kind?

Do I struggle to master matters that test all of my resources?

Can I stand and profit by severe criticism when I have been or seem to have been at fault?

Do I, if necessary, court severe discipline as a preparatory course for a desired vocation or do I pamper myself and like to be coddled by others?

Do I strive for personal efficiency, grasp at opportunities and recognize my right to advancement?

Do I rebound quickly from defeat?

Am I indifferent to supercilious fault-finding?

Do I enjoy being in contests of fortitude and endurance and in intellectual combats?

If I were a candidate for some elective office would defeat dishearten me or should I reckon each successive defeat as preparation for final victory?

When confronted with unexpected difficulties in anything that I have undertaken, is my first impulse, or reaction, the desire to back down or to go ahead with greater energy than before?

Do I stand by the presumption that I am to succeed, even when things look blackest?

Have I a persistent resolution when once a careful judgment has been made?

In making purchases—whether of neckties or machinery equipments—do I inspect the goods under consideration and form independent opinion of their merits or am I influenced unconsciously in my decisions by what I think the salesman may think of me?

Do I sometimes accept less than I know I should for services rendered because I lack the stamina to stand up for my rights?

"Resolve to perform what you ought; perform without fail what you resolve." —Benjamin Franklin

A Stout Heart
FROM *SELF-HELP*, 1876
By Samuel Smiles

The cultivation of this quality is of the greatest importance; resolute determination in the pursuit of worthy objects being the foundation of all true greatness of character. Energy enables a man to force his way through irksome drudgery and dry details, and carries him onward and upward in every station in life. It accomplishes more than genius, with not one-half the disappointment and peril. It is not eminent talent that is required to ensure success in any pursuit, so much as purpose—not merely the power to achieve, but the will to labour energetically and perseveringly.

Hence energy of will may be defined to be the very central power of character in a man—in a word, it is the Man himself. It gives impulse to his every action, and soul to every effort. True hope is based on it—and it is hope that gives the real perfume to life. There is a fine heraldic motto on a broken helmet in Battle Abbey, "L'espoir est ma force" ["Hope is my strength"], which might be the motto of every man's life. "Woe unto him that is faint-hearted," says the son of Sirach. There is, indeed, no blessing equal to the possession of a stout heart. Even if a man fail in his efforts, it will be a great satisfaction to him to enjoy the consciousness of having done his best. In humble life nothing can be more cheering and beautiful than to see a man combating suffering by patience, triumphing in his integrity, and who, when his feet are bleeding and his limbs failing him, still walks upon his courage.

"The block of granite which is an obstacle in the pathway of the weak, becomes a stepping-stone in the pathway of the strong." —Thomas Carlyle

How Are You Playing the Game?
By Anonymous

Life is a game with a glorious prize,
If we can only play it right.
It is give and take, build and break,
And often it ends in a fight;
But he surely wins who honestly tries
(Regardless of wealth or fame),
He can never despair who plays it fair
How are you playing the game?

Do you wilt and whine, if you fail to win
In the manner you think your due?
Do you sneer at the man in case
    that he can
And does, do better than you?
Do you take your rebuffs with a
    knowing grin?
Do you laugh tho' you pull up lame?
Does your faith hold true when the
    whole world's blue?
How are you playing the game?

Get into the thick of it—wade in, boys!
Whatever your cherished goal;
Brace up your will till your pulses thrill,
And you dare to your very soul!
Do something more than make a noise;
Let your purpose leap into flame
As you plunge with a cry, "I shall do or die,"
Then you will be playing the game.

"An acorn is not an oak when it is sprouted. It must go through long summers and fierce winters, and endure all that frost, and snow, and thunder, and storms, and side-striking winds can bring, before it is a full grown oak. So a man is not a man when he is created; he is only begun. His manhood must come with years. He who goes through life prosperous, and comes to his grave without a wrinkle, is not half a man. Difficulties are God's errands and trainers, and only through them can one come to fullness of manhood." —Henry Ward Beecher

The Man in the Arena

FROM THE SPEECH, *CITIZENSHIP IN A REPUBLIC*, 1910
By Theodore Roosevelt

It is not the critic who counts; not the man who points out how the strong man stumbles, or where the doer of deeds could have done them better. The credit belongs to the man who is actually in the arena, whose face is marred by dust and sweat and blood; who strives valiantly; who errs, who comes short again and again, because there is no effort without error and shortcoming; but who does actually strive to do the deeds; who knows great enthusiasms, the great devotions; who spends himself in a worthy cause; who at the best knows in the end the triumph of high achievement, and who at the worst, if he fails, at least fails while daring greatly, so that his place shall never be with those cold and timid souls who neither know victory nor defeat.

> *"Resolve, resolve, and to be men aspire.*
> *Exert that noblest privilege, alone,*
> *Here to mankind indulged; control desire:*
> *Let god-like reason, from her sovereign throne,*
> *Speak the commanding word 'I will!' and it is done."*
> **—James Thomson**

Determination Is the Answer

From *WE WHO ARE ALIVE AND REMAIN: UNTOLD STORIES FROM THE BAND OF BROTHERS*, 2009
By Marcus Brotherton

The story of the Band of Brothers, World War II's Easy Company, 506th Parachute Infantry Regiment, 101st Airborne Division, has in recent times been made famous by historian Stephen Ambrose's book and the HBO miniseries which chronicled their legendary exploits. It is a story that embodies and speaks to every quality of true manliness; while the men would never call themselves such, they are truly modern-day heroes.

After parachute drops and fighting in D-Day and Operation Market Garden, the men of Easy Company were sent to Mourmelon, France, for some much needed R&R. But less than two weeks later they were called to defend the Belgian town of Bastogne as part of the larger Battle of the Bulge. Having to quickly move out, the men were severely lacking in ammunition, winter clothing, and other supplies. Surrounded by German troops, the men dug in for an intense fight in the bitter cold. Having arrived on December 17, 1945, it would be a long month before Easy Company was pulled off the line and given hot food, showers, and a few days rest.

For Easy Company men like Clancy Lyall, Herb Suerth Jr., and Bill Wingett, Bastogne was the ultimate test of their hardihood and resolve; their experiences put the little annoyances that bother us each day in proper perspective.

CLANCY LYALL

We made our defensive perimeter in the Bois Jacques woods. The next day we woke up and a snow was coming down like you never saw. I was wearing my same old green jumpsuit—it wasn't designed to keep out the cold. I had an M-1 and a bandolier, a few K rations, a field jacket, and a towel around my neck. After a while I was able to find an overcoat. I took one from a dead GI, one of ours, an infantry guy.

To stay warm you got close to each other. You can't make fires. If you're lucky enough to have a blanket, it gets wet so it doesn't do much good. You never take your boots off and leave them off. If you do, your feet freeze up. In the nighttime we went on patrols, so those help you stay warm. You never really sleep; you get two, three cat winks then hear a round and that wakes you up. You got used to going without sleep. After a while you can walk sleeping.

For shelter, we found tree limbs to put over our foxholes. I knew guys who put frozen German corpses over the top of their holes to insulate against the cold. I never did. Your hands got so cold, guys urinated on their hands to warm them up. You did the same thing with your M-1. If your bolt was stuck, it wouldn't fire. What the hell are you going to have it for then? So guys pissed on their rifles, jacked the bolt back a couple of times, and it was all right.

You couldn't shower. You were so dirty you smelled a guy from twenty yards away. But everybody smelled the same, so what the hell. There was only one time in my life I smelled worse. Years later, in Korea, I jumped and landed in a rice paddy. They had put human feces in there and I landed in that sonuvabitch. I bathed and I bathed but it took me months to get rid of the smell. It was like a skunk had sprayed me.

One day in Bastogne I got hit. I had no place to go. It was just a graze across my forehead. Maybe a little bit better than a graze—it put a line across my skull. They bandaged me up at an aid station. I got a cup of hot coffee and spent the night. The next day I was back in my foxhole.

Things got a bit shaky around that time. I have to say something at this point: airborne outfits that go into combat are supposed to be relieved within three to five days. But it never happened; not with us, anyway. Normandy was thirty-four days combat. Holland was seventy-four days combat. When we got to Mourmelon, it was right into battle again. By the time we got into Bastogne, we were all flaky to start with. Then we were forty days combat in Bastogne. If it wasn't for each other, I'm sure a lot of us would have gone crazy. That's where the cohesion comes in. We were brothers.

HERB SUERTH JR.

Bastogne was the coldest place I've ever been in my life. My wife and I have a cabin up in Wisconsin today where we often spend some time in winters, and even now, sitting in the warmth of that cabin, I'll look out at the snow covered pine trees and shiver. It's just a reaction.

A lot of the struggle in Bastogne was trying to keep your feet dry and warm. It was a twenty-four-hour-a-day exercise. If you weren't vigilant you had trench foot within hours. I was a bit lucky because I had been previously issued galoshes, rubber overshoes, with clips. They weren't perfect. Your feet would sweat in them because they were enclosed, and get wet from the inside out. But they did keep the snow off and keep your feet from being soaked from the outside in. I never wore the burlap bags a lot of the guys put on their feet.

If you changed your socks three to four times a day, you could keep your feet pretty dry. You dried your socks with body heat by putting them in your helmet or wrapping them around your waist. I had six to eight pairs of socks. I kept them with me all the time and never put them back in my personal bag. You wouldn't wash them—hell, no; you just dried them. It was hard to get water because you had to melt snow to get it, and fires were too dangerous. You couldn't even keep water in your canteen at night because it froze. One of the things I learned back at the Blue Ridge [in training] was to always have a needle and thread with me to repair gloves. That proved handy at Bastogne because your gloves stuck to the rifle barrels and ripped because of the cold.

I was wounded when an artillery round landed next to me. Both my legs were broken. I spent three months in skeletal traction. They drill a hole through your knee, put a wire through all the bones, then put a U-shaped brace over that. At the end of that brace they hook up a wire. That goes up over the end of the bed and puts weights on it to keep your legs straight. Talk about painful. You've got to realize that by now all of us have tremendous leg muscles. We've been running, hiking, climbing, exercising—it takes a lot of weight to overcome your thigh muscles so the bones can set properly. If you ever want to interrogate an enemy soldier, just put him in skeletal traction. About the third day he'll tell you anything you want.

They used maggots on my legs to eat away the dead flesh. I guessed it worked, because I kept my legs. At one point they had talked about amputating them. Altogether, I was in the hospital for eighteen months—three months in traction, then another six months in bed, then months of rehabilitation after that. It took a long time before I could set a foot on the floor. The first day I did, I stood up. The next day after that I walked across the damn hospital floor on a pair of rolling parallel bars. Ten days later I was out on a weekend pass. They fitted me for a set of braces that I wore for about three months after that. I worked at rehab eight hours a day until I finally healed.

BILL WINGETT

Just back from the hospital in Brussels, I pulled into Mourmelon one-and-a-half days before we piled on trucks for Bastogne. We drove for quite a while, we only got off the truck for piss call—I think we only did that twice. I didn't have hardly any of my equipment. When our guys were coming south when we were coming north, I never hesitated saying, "Hey, I need that." So I got to Bastogne with a couple of good coats and a rifle, borrowed from the guys who were retreating.

After some time I had to go to the infirmary for my feet because they were frozen. They were shelling the infirmary while I was there. But I was never shot. I was one of the few. Did I ever think I was going to die? I can only remember a couple of times thinking "this might be it." But I do not remember any time that I felt like hunkering down in a foxhole and covering up my head in fear. Understand this: I'm not a religious person. I believe in God. I'll say more than that—I *know* there's a God. And I know that there's got to be several occasions I displeased God, whatever form He's in. But I never felt the need to get down on my knees and pray that I wouldn't die. I don't think it ever crossed my mind that I wasn't going home—not while I was in a foxhole, not while sitting on the line somewhere. I always figured tomorrow was coming and I was going to be there. I never had a doubt that I wouldn't go home.

Early in our training, it could have been Sink, or Sobel, or Winters, somebody said, "Determination is the answer." I took that to heart. At Bastogne we were cold. We were hungry. But we had to get the job done. A job ought to be done right if you're going to do it at all.

Ulysses

FROM *POEMS*, 1842
By Alfred, Lord Tennyson

• •

The Odyssey, written by the Greek poet Homer, follows the hero Odysseus (Ulysses in Roman myths) as he journeys home after fighting in the Trojan War. After ten years of fighting, Odysseus was determined to return to his family as quickly as possible. But he is thwarted in his quest by obstacles and monsters, and it takes him another decade of traveling to make it back to Ithaca. During that time Odysseus never wavers in his resolve to embrace his family once more.

In "Ulysses," Tennyson imagines life for Odysseus after the euphoria of his homecoming has waned and life in Ithaca has returned to normal. Odysseus is advanced in years and free from his former hardships, and yet is restless for further challenge and travel on the open seas; he resolves to die living a life of adventure and prepares to set sail once again. Tennyson wrote this poem after learning of the death of his close friend and fellow poet, Arthur Henry Hallam. Devastated by the loss of this companion, Tennyson said the poem "gave my feeling about the need of going forward and braving the struggle of life," that despite such loss, "still life must be fought out to the end."

• •

It little profits that an idle king,
By this still hearth, among these barren crags,
Matched with an aged wife, I mete and dole
Unequal laws unto a savage race,
That hoard, and sleep, and feed, and know not me.
I cannot rest from travel: I will drink
Life to the lees: all times I have enjoy'd
Greatly, have suffer'd greatly, both with those
That loved me, and alone; on shore, and when
Thro' scudding drifts the rainy Hyades

Vext the dim sea: I am become a name.

For always roaming with a hungry heart

Much have I seen and known: cities of men,

And manners, climates, councils, governments,

Myself not least, but honour'd of them all;

And drunk delight of battle with my peers,

Far on the ringing plains of windy Troy.

I am part of all that I have met;

Yet all experience is an arch wherethro'

Gleams that untravell'd world, whose margin fades

For ever and for ever when I move.

How dull it is to pause, to make an end,

To rust unburnish'd, not to shine in use!

As tho' to breathe were life. Life piled on life

Where all too little, and of one to me

Little remains: but every hour is saved

From that eternal silence, something more,

A bringer of new things; and vile it were

For some three suns to store and hoard myself,

And this gray spirit yearning in desire

To follow knowledge like a sinking star,
Beyond the utmost bound of human thought.

This is my son, my own Telemachus,
To whom I leave the sceptre and the isle—
Well-loved of me, discerning to fulfil
This labour, by slow prudence to make mild
A rugged people, and thro' soft degrees
Subdue them to the useful and the good.
Most blameless is he, centered in the sphere
Of common duties, decent not to fail
In offices of tenderness, and pay
Meet adoration to my household gods,
When I am gone. He works his work, I mine.
There lies the port; the vessel puffs her sail:
There gloom the dark broad seas. My mariners,
Souls that have toil'd, and wrought, and thought with me—
That ever with a frolic welcome took
The thunder and the sunshine, and opposed
Free hearts, free foreheads—you and I are old;
Old age hath yet his honour and his toil;
Death closes all: but something ere the end,
Some work of noble note, may yet be done,
Not unbecoming men that strove with gods.
The lights begin to twinkle from the rocks;
The long day wanes: the slow moon climbs: the deep
Moans round with many voices. Come, my friends.
'Tis not too late to seek a newer world.
Push off, and sitting well in order smite
The sounding furrows; for my purpose holds
To sail beyond the sunset, and the baths
Of all the western stars, until I die.

It may be that the gulfs will wash us down;
It may be that we shall touch the Happy Isles,
And see the great Achilles, whom we knew;
Tho' much is taken, much abides; and tho'
We are not now that strength which in old days
Moved earth and heaven; that which we are, we are;
One equal temper of heroic hearts,
Made weak by time and fate, but strong in will
To strive, to seek, to find, and not to yield.

"There is nothing more to be esteemed than a manly firmness and decision of character." —William Hazlitt

A Highly Developed Power of Choosing
FROM *THE BUSINESS PHILOSOPHER*, 1909

Of the two elements constituting Will—choice and that persistence of effort which brings about a realization of the choice—we need to note in reference to a highly developed power of choosing several important characteristics. *First*, the capability to actually make a choice—a decisive, fixed, definite choice. So far as possible, the choice should be consciously made. We should realize that we are rendering a decision—consciously linking our lives in the chain of destiny.

Second, the choice, when made, should represent our *actual feelings*. It should be the expression of our predominant desires. I hold that the Will, in choosing, should be a servant and not a dictator, a slave and not a master.

Third, having chosen one of several alternatives, all the rest should be *banished* from the mind. The man of developed power of choice may hesitate long; yet having picked one plan from the many, the many will be forgotten. His mind is now as free from their influence as if they never had been. Doubt is over. Hesitancy is over. "The die is cast."

And here we have one of the great psychic elements which distinguishes the man of executive ability from the common man. That foe to all action—regret—does not reach him. He will hesitate, doubt, compare, discriminate, speculate, and reconsider *before* a choice is made—but not afterwards. But the man of inferior executive ability—though having made a decision, though having picked his course—keeps on comparing, deciding, doubting, and picking. And though having decided over and over many times, he still hesitates in the execution for fear of a mistake in the planning, for fear that he has blundered in the choice.

THE EXECUTIVE QUALITY

But the man with a trained will, having decided once, never turns back—never reconsiders. He says to his memory in reference to any other choice he might have made "forget it." Before making the choice he saw many roads that he might take. But after making it he sees but one.

Fourth, having made a choice, having decided upon a plan, we must have the courage to *stand by it.* The man of high executive ability is not terrified, as is the average man, by the fact of a mistake—and the probability of more to follow. He is not frightened to death because of a failure. Defeat to him is nothing more than delay.

Does the successful man never make mistakes? He does. Does he never choose the wrong course? Sometimes. Does he never blunder in his decisions? Often. How, then, does he succeed? First, by having a *predominance* of correct decisions. Second, by enforcing these with unerring precision and celerity of movement.

SUPPOSE YOU BLUNDER?

Your man of high executive ability, of developed power of choice, of keen capacity in the forming of a plan, knows that he will make many mistakes, many blunders, many errors, many bad decisions. He knows that after the work is all done he will see numerous places where it could have been better. But what of it? Life is as much in the striving as in the gaining, in the effort as in the reward, in the sowing as in the reaping.

NO REGRETS

The successful man knows but little of regrets, cares but little for past failures, and broods but little over the blunders he has made. And he could not be successful if he did.

And yet it is not because he never fell down that he is now up, but simply because he would not stay down. It may have been another's fault that he fell. It would have been his own had he lain there. His final success came not because he did not blunder, but because he did not keep his attention constantly on his blunders. He dwelt upon these simply long enough to find the cause, so as not to make the same mistake twice. Once is enough. One should have variety even in his blunders.

A *fifth* characteristic of the power of a developed choice is *definiteness*. A plan clearly, vividly, and intensely conceived is already half executed. The choice must not only be decisive but *incisive*. When the plan lacks the quality of definiteness, when it is uncertain, vague and foggy—indistinct in outline and uncertain as to detail—a swift and vigorous execution is impossible. And so before there can be speed and accuracy of execution, there must be *definiteness of planning*. And the more definite, distinct, exact, and clear-cut the choice or decision, the easier its execution. A plan of action possessing such qualities will almost execute itself.

THE VALUE OF PROMPTNESS

A *sixth* characteristic of a developed power to choose is *promptness* of decision. While the whole field should be carefully surveyed before the choice is made, while every alternative should be examined and the possibilities of each considered; yet it must be recognized that *time* is an element in the making of a choice. All things are in motion. Even the planet on which we live, and the sun around which it revolves, is moving. Our time is always *limited*. Even life is limited. And on many a hard-fought field *promptness of decision* turned defeat into victory.

I think it holds true that men possessing great promptness and decisiveness of decision were men strongly given to *meditation*. They had the imaginative power to picture nearly all possible contingencies, and thus to decide beforehand what they would do under each one. Their prompt decisions were the product of premeditation. In their solitary wanderings and musings they were picturing, dreaming, speculating, conjecturing as to the possibilities which might arise. And so to have promptness of decision accompanied by accuracy, there must be forethought and premeditation.

And yet I must recognize the fact that we always have the extremes. Every important law of life is a contradiction—a paradox. It always requires the possession of two conflicting processes. And so it is here. At the one extreme is the man who does not reflect in advance. He seizes upon the first plan which comes into his mind, forms a definite, fixed, unchangeable resolution, and proceeds immediately to action—and to vigorous action at that. His decisions are made quickly, and his action follows instantly. If the choice happens to be right, he "wins big." If it happens to be wrong, he is "down and out." Here we have promptness of decision. But it lacks in accuracy and reliability.

REFLECT NOT TOO MUCH

At the other extreme is the man who reflects long and often, who takes everything into consideration, who goes over the whole field—not once but many times; who pictures every possibility, every contingency, and every danger arising from each course. He considers not simply one plan but many plans. But the trouble is that he has taken so many things into consideration, has pictured so many different plans, and sees so many different ways by which it could be done, that he cannot decide upon any. The difference between them is so slight that he has no preference. And without a preference there cannot be a choice. But the great executive character has the will to make a choice when no preference exists. And so he is a combination of the powers and capacities of both—with the defects of neither.

The *seventh*, and last, trait of a developed power of choosing to be here mentioned, is that the choice, or plan, when made, must be *immovable*. The choice must become a permanent part of the nervous system, a fixed structure of the brain. The choice, the plan, the resolution, must be fixed, firm, substantial—immovable.

The decision, when made, must be formed of such firmness of mental fiber that it will not dissolve into fragments and shreds when nervous energy is poured into it. It must be able to withstand the conflicts of contending emotions and weather the storms of passion intact.

Some people's plans, decisions, and resolutions are but little more than "dissolving views." And yet it is only when a determination has solidified and crystallized into a *conviction* that it can be made the foundation for great achievements.

"People do not lack strength; they lack will." —Victor Hugo

The Quitter
FROM *RHYMES OF A ROLLING STONE*, 1912
By Robert Service

When you're lost in the Wild, and you're scared as a child,
And Death looks you bang in the eye,
And you're sore as a boil, it's according to Hoyle
To cock your revolver and … die.
But the Code of a Man says: "Fight all you can,"
And self-dissolution is barred.
In hunger and woe, oh, it's easy to blow …
It's the hell-served-for-breakfast that's hard.

"You're sick of the game!" Well, now, that's a shame.
You're young and you're brave and you're bright.
"You've had a raw deal!" I know—but don't squeal,
Buck up, do your damnedest, and fight.
It's the plugging away that will win you the day,
So don't be a piker, old pard!
Just draw on your grit; it's so easy to quit:
It's the keeping-your-chin-up that's hard.

It's easy to cry that you're beaten—and die;
It's easy to crawfish and crawl;
But to fight and to fight when hope's out of sight—
Why, that's the best game of them all!
And though you come out of each grueling bout,
All broken and beaten and scarred,
Just have one more try—it's dead easy to die,
It's the keeping-on-living that's hard.

"And having thus chosen our course, without guile and with pure purpose, let us renew our trust in God and go forward without fear and with manly hearts." —Abraham Lincoln

To Fight It to the Last
THE FINAL LETTER OF ROBERT FALCON SCOTT TO HIS WIFE
FROM THE SOUTH POLE, 1912

In January of 1912, Englishman Robert Falcon Scott, along with a team of four others, began the last leg of their quest to become the first men to reach the South Pole. The hopes of these intrepid explorers were dashed when they neared their destination only to find that Roald Amundsen had gotten there before them. Incredibly dejected, the men now faced a wearisome eight-hundred-mile return journey.

The men trudged forward day after day, through the snow and ice, battling 70-degrees-below-zero temperatures and blinding blizzards. Dwindling rations and frostbite sapped the men's strength and spirit. One of the five men, Edgar Evans, collapsed and died. Another, Lawrence "Titus" Oates, could no longer go on, but the team refused to leave him behind. Choosing to sacrifice himself to improve the other men's chances of survival, he simply left his tent and walked away, telling the others, "I am just going outside and may be some time." He was never seen again. Scott wrote, "We knew that poor Oates was walking to his death, but though we tried to dissuade him, we knew it was the act of a brave man and an English gentleman."

Stuck in a blizzard with dwindling supplies, the men knew the end was nigh for them as well. No longer able to continue the march, the men hunkered down and prepared for death. Despite the bitter cold and incredible fatigue, Scott managed to write twelve letters to his family and friends, to the relatives of the other men on the team, and to his fellow countrymen. In a "Message to the Public," Scott chalked the expedition's failure up to unfortunate circumstances and ended by saying:

> "But for my own sake I do not regret this journey, which has shown that Englishmen can endure hardships, help one another, and meet death with as great a fortitude as ever in the past. We took risks, we knew we took them; things have come out against us, and therefore we have no cause for complaint, but bow to the will of providence, determined still to do our best to the last. ... Had we lived, I should have had a tale to tell of the hardihood, endurance, and courage of my companions which would have stirred the heart of every Englishman. These rough notes and our dead bodies must tell the tale."

The men died ten days later. They were found frozen in their sleeping bags. Although the explorers carried lethal doses of opium and morphine, which would have enabled them to end their suffering and take their own lives, these supplies remained untouched.

The following is the letter Scott wrote to Kathleen, his wife and the mother of their three-year-old son, Peter. She did not receive it until the doomed explorer's body was found in 1913.

Note: The punctuation and format of the letter has been slightly edited. Scott struggled to write the letter in subzero temperatures over the course of several days, scribbling his thoughts as best he could, filling several pages, and then writing across the backs of the paper. The letter ends abruptly and without a signature.

. . . .

To My Widow

Dearest darling – We are in a very tight corner and I have doubts of pulling through – In one short lunch hour I take advantage of a very small measure of warmth to write letters preparatory to a possible end – The first is naturally to you on whom my thoughts mostly dwell waking or sleeping – If anything happens to me I shall like you to know how much you have meant to me and what pleasant recollections are with me as I depart –

I should like you to take what comfort you can from these facts also – I shall not have suffered any pain but leave the world fresh from harness & full of good health & vigour – this is decided already – when provisions come to an end we Simply stop unless we are within easy distance of another depot –Therefore you must not imagine a great tragedy – we are very anxious of course & have been for weeks but our splendid physical condition and our appetites compensate for all discomfort – The cold is trying & sometimes angering but here again the hot food which drives it forth is so wonderfully enjoyable that one would scarcely be without it.

We have gone down hill a good deal since I wrote the above – Poor Titus Oates has gone – he was in a bad state. The rest of us keep going and imagine we have a chance to get through but the cold weather doesn't let up at all. We are now only 20 miles from a depot but we have very little food & fuel

Well dear heart I want you to take the whole thing very sensibly as I'm sure you will. The boy will be your comfort. I had looked forward to helping you to bring him up but it is a satisfaction to feel that he is safe with you. I think both he and you ought to be specially looked after by the country for which after all we have given our lives with something of spirit which makes for example – I am writing letters on this point in the end of this book after this. Will you send them to their various destinations? I must write a little letter for the boy if time can be found to be read when he grows up. The inherited vice from my side of the family is indolence – above all he must guard & you must guard him against that. Make him a strenuous man. I had to force myself into being strenuous, as you know – had always an inclination to be idle, my father was idle and it brought much trouble.

Dearest that you know I cherish no sentimental rubbish about re marriage – when the right man comes to help you in life you ought to be your happy self again – I wasn't a very good husband but I hope I shall be a good memory – certainly the end is nothing for you to be ashamed of and I like to think that the boy will have a good start in parentage of which he may be proud.

Dear it is not easy to write because of the cold – 70 degrees below zero and nothing but the shelter of our tent – you know I have loved you, you know my thoughts must have constantly dwelt on you and oh dear me you must know that quite the worst aspect of this situation is the thought that I shall not see you again – The inevitable must be faced – you urged me to be leader of this party and I know you felt it would be dangerous – I've taken my place throughout, haven't I? God bless you my own darling – I shall try and write more later – I go on across the back pages

Since writing the above we have got to within 11 miles of our depot with one hot meal and two days cold food and we should have got through but have been held for four days by a frightful storm – I think the best chance has gone. We have decided not to kill ourselves but to fight it to the last for that depot but in the fighting there is a painless end so don't worry.

I have written letters on odd pages of this book – will you manage to get them sent? You see I am anxious for you and the boy's future – make the boy interested in natural history if you can, it is better than games – they encourage it at some schools – I know you will keep him out in the open air – try and make him believe in a God, it is comforting.

Oh my dear my dear what dreams I have had of his future and yet oh my girl I know you will face it stoically – your portrait and the boy's will be found in my breast and the one in the little red Morocco case given by Lady Baxter – There is a piece of the Union flag I put up at the South Pole in my private kit bag together with Amundsen's black flag and other trifles – give a small piece of the Union flag to the King and a small piece to Queen Alexandra and keep the rest a poor trophy for you!

What lots and lots I could tell you of this journey. How much better it has been than lounging in too great comfort at home – what tales you would have for the boy but oh what a price to pay – to forfeit the sight of your dear dear face – Dear you will be good to the old mother. I write her a little line in this book. Also keep in with Ettie and the others – oh but you'll put on a strong face for the world – only don't be too proud to accept help for the boys sake – he ought to have a fine career and do something in the world. I haven't time to write to Sir Clements – tell him I thought much of him and never regretted him putting me in command of the Discovery. – Give messages of farewell to Lady Baxter and Lady Sandhurst keep friends with them for both are dear women & to also both the Reginald Smiths

> *"Stand firm and immovable as an anvil when it is beaten upon."* **—Saint Ignatius**

The Man With the Iron Will

FROM *BALLADS OF THE HEARTHSTONE*, 1901
By Henry H. Johnson

Give me the man with an iron will

And a purpose firm and strong;—

Who dares to stand by the right until

He has crushed to death the wrong;

Who treads where the path of duty leads,

Though the way be blocked by foes;—

Whose heart and hand a good cause speeds,

No matter who oppose.

Give me the man with an iron will,

Who knows no such word as fail;

Who will, if need, his heart's blood spill

To make the *good* prevail;

Who guards the right with his strong arm,

And dares to stand 'gainst might;

Who shields the poor and weak from harm,
And does right because *'tis* right.

Give me the man with an iron will
And a heart as true as gold;—
Whose God-given mission he will fulfill,
Who cannot be bought nor sold.
Give me the man whom no power can bend
From a purpose grand and high;—
Whose all, for a righteous cause will spend,
For a righteous cause will die.

Let No Feeling of Discouragement Prey Upon You

A Letter from Abraham Lincoln to George Latham, 1860

Abraham Lincoln wrote the following letter to George Latham, who was a close friend of Lincoln's son Robert. Both young men hoped to attend Harvard. Robert passed the entrance exams; George did not. George's father had died several years before, and Lincoln wrote to George with paternal concern and as a man who knew something about perseverance.

Springfield, Ills. July 22, 1860

My dear George

I have scarcely felt greater pain in my life than on learning yesterday from Bob's letter, that you failed to enter Harvard University. And yet there is very little in it, if you will allow no feeling of *discouragement* to seize, and prey upon you. It is a *certain* truth, that you *can* enter, and graduate in, Harvard University; and having made the attempt, you *must* succeed in it. *"Must"* is the word.

I know not how to aid you, save in the assurance of one of mature age, and much severe experience, that you *can* not fail, if you resolutely determine, that you *will* not.

The President of the institution, can scarcely be other than a kind man; and doubtless he would grant you an interview, and point out the readiest way to remove, or overcome, the obstacles which have thwarted you.

In your temporary failure there is no evidence that you may not yet be a better scholar, and a more successful man in the great struggle of life, than many others, who have entered college more easily.

Again I say let no feeling of discouragement prey upon you, and in the end you are sure to succeed.

With more than a common interest I subscribe myself.

Very truly your friend,
A. Lincoln.

For a Man Cannot Know Himself Without a Trial
FROM THE ESSAY "ON PROVIDENCE," IN *THE MINOR DIALOGUES*, C. 60–65 A.D.
By Seneca

• •

In this essay, Seneca gives the Stoic explanation for why the gods allow bad things to happen to good people. His answer? What seems like hardship is really for our good; adversity tests and strengthens us and allows us to demonstrate our virtue.

• •

Prosperity comes to the mob, and to low-minded men as well as to great ones; but it is the privilege of great men alone to send under the yoke the disasters and terrors of mortal life: whereas to be always prosperous, and to pass through life without a twinge of mental distress, is to remain ignorant of one half of nature. You are a great man; but how am I to know it, if fortune gives you no opportunity of showing your virtue?

You have entered the arena of the Olympic games, but no one else has done so: you have the crown, but not the victory: I do not congratulate you as I would a brave man, but as one who has obtained a consulship or praetorship. You have gained dignity. I may say the same of a good man, if troublesome circumstances have never given him a single opportunity of displaying the strength of his mind. I think you unhappy because you never have been unhappy: you have passed through your life without meeting an antagonist: no one will know your powers, not even you yourself.

For a man cannot know himself without a trial: no one ever learnt what he could do without putting himself to the test; for which reason many have of their own free will exposed themselves to misfortunes which no longer came in their way, and have sought for an opportunity of making their virtue, which otherwise would have been lost in darkness, shine before the world. Great men, I say, often rejoice at crosses of fortune just as brave soldiers do at wars. I remember to have heard Triumphus, who was a gladiator in the reign of Tiberius Caesar, complaining about the scarcity of prizes. "What a glorious time," said he, "is past."

Valour is greedy of danger, and thinks only of whither it strives to go, not of what it will suffer, since even what it will suffer is part of its glory. Soldiers pride themselves on their wounds, they joyously display their blood flowing over their breastplate. Though those who return unwounded from battle may have done as bravely, yet he who returns wounded is more admired.

Do not, I beg you, dread those things which the immortal gods apply to our minds like spurs: misfortune is virtue's opportunity. Those men may justly be called unhappy who are stupified with excess of enjoyment, whom sluggish contentment keeps as it were becalmed in a quiet sea: whatever befalls them will come strange to them. Misfortunes press hardest on those who are unacquainted with them: the yoke feels heavy to the tender neck. The recruit turns pale at the thought of a wound: the veteran, who knows that he has often won the victory after losing blood, looks boldly at his own flowing gore.

Avoid luxury, avoid effeminate enjoyment, by which men's minds are softened, and in which, unless something occurs to remind them of the common lot of humanity, they lie unconscious, as though plunged in continual drunkenness. He whom glazed windows have always guarded from the wind, whose feet are warmed by constantly renewed fomentations, whose dining-room is heated by hot air beneath the floor and spread through the walls, cannot meet the gentlest breeze without danger. While all excesses are hurtful, excess of comfort is the most hurtful of all; it affects the brain; it leads men's minds into vain imaginings; it spreads a thick cloud over the boundaries of truth and falsehood.

Why then should we wonder if God tries noble spirits severely? There can be no easy proof of virtue. Fortune lashes and mangles us: well, let us endure it: it is not cruelty, it is a struggle, in which the oftener we engage the braver we shall become. The strongest part of the body is that which is

CHAPTER FOUR

exercised by the most frequent use: we must entrust ourselves to fortune to be hardened by her against herself: by degrees she will make us a match for herself. Familiarity with danger leads us to despise it. Thus the bodies of sailors are hardened by endurance of the sea, and the hands of farmers by work; the arms of soldiers are powerful to hurl darts, the legs of runners are active: that part of each man which he exercises is the strongest.

No tree which the wind does not often blow against is firm and strong; for it is stiffened by the very act of being shaken, and plants its roots more securely: those which grow in a sheltered valley are brittle: and so it is to the advantage of good men, and causes them to be undismayed, that they should live much amidst alarms, and learn to bear with patience what is not evil save to him who endures it ill.

"Fight one more round. When your arms are so tired that you can hardly lift your hands to come on guard, fight one more round. When your nose is bleeding and your eyes are black and you are so tired that you wish your opponent would crack you one on the jaw and put you to sleep, fight one more round—remembering that the man who fights one more round is never whipped." —James "Gentleman Jim" Corbett, heavyweight boxing champion

The Fighter
By S.E. Kiser

I fight a battle every day
Against discouragement and fear;
Some foe stands always in my way,
The path ahead is never clear!

I must forever be on guard
Against the doubts that skulk along;
I get ahead by fighting hard,
But fighting keeps my spirit strong.

I hear the croakings of Despair,
The dark predictions of the weak;
I find myself pursued by Care,
No matter what the end I seek;
My victories are small and few,
It matters not how hard I strive;
Each day the fight begins anew,
But fighting keeps my hopes alive.

My dreams are spoiled by circumstance,
My plans are wrecked by Fate or Luck;
Some hour, perhaps, will bring my chance,
But that great hour has never struck;
My progress has been slow and hard,
I've had to climb and crawl and swim,
Fighting for every stubborn yard,
But I have kept in fighting trim.

I have to fight my doubts away,
And be on guard against my fears;
The feeble croaking of Dismay
Has been familiar through the years;
My dearest plans keep going wrong,
Events combine to thwart my will,
But fighting keeps my spirit strong,
And I am undefeated still!

The Last of the Human Freedoms— to Choose One's Own Way

FROM *MAN'S SEARCH FOR MEANING*, 1959
By Viktor Frankl

In 1942, Jewish psychiatrist Viktor Emil Frankl, along with his wife and parents, were taken to the Theresienstadt concentration camp. There Frankl put his expertise to use in helping other prisoners deal with their grief and despair. At the same time, his own suffering led him to explore the meaning of life and how to find that meaning even in the midst of soul-crushing adversity.

In spite of all the enforced physical and mental primitiveness of the life in a concentration camp, it was possible for spiritual life to deepen. Sensitive people who were used to a rich intellectual life may have suffered much pain (they were often of a delicate constitution), but the damage to their inner selves was less. They were able to retreat from their terrible surroundings to a life of inner riches and spiritual freedom. Only in this way can one explain the apparent paradox that some prisoners of a less hardy makeup often seemed to survive camp life better than did those of a robust nature. In order to make myself clear, I am forced to fall back on personal experience. Let me tell what happened on those early mornings when we had to march to our work site.

There were shouted commands: "Detachment, forward march! Left-2-3-4! Left-2-3-4! Left-2-3-4! Left-2-3-4! First man about, left and left and left and left! Caps off!" These words sound in my ears even now. At the order "Caps off!" we passed the gate of the camp, and searchlights were trained upon us. Whoever did not march smartly got a kick. And worse off was the man who, because of the cold, had pulled his cap back over his ears before permission was given.

We stumbled on in the darkness, over big stones and through large puddles, along the one road leading from the camp. The accompanying guards kept shouting at us and driving us with the butts of their rifles. Anyone with very sore feet supported himself on his neighbor's arm. Hardly a word was spoken; the icy wind did not encourage talk. Hiding his mouth behind his upturned collar, the man marching next to me whispered suddenly: "If our wives could see us now! I do hope they are better off in their camps and don't know what is happening to us."

That brought thoughts of my own wife to mind. And as we stumbled on for miles, slipping on icy spots, supporting each other time and again, dragging one another up and onward, nothing was said, but we both knew: each of us was thinking of his wife. Occasionally I looked at the sky, where the stars were fading and the pink light of the morning was beginning to spread behind a dark bank of clouds. But my mind clung to my wife's image, imagining it with an uncanny acuteness. I heard her answering me, saw her smile, her frank and encouraging look. Real or not, her look was then more luminous than the sun which was beginning to rise.

A thought transfixed me: for the first time in my life I saw the truth as it is set into song by so many poets, proclaimed as the final wisdom by so many thinkers. The truth—that love is the ultimate and the highest goal to which man can aspire. Then I grasped the meaning of the greatest secret that human poetry and human thought and belief have to impart: *The salvation of man is through love and in love.* I understood how a man who has nothing left in this world still may know bliss, be it only for a brief moment, in the contemplation of his beloved. In a position of utter desolation, when man cannot express himself in positive action, when his only achievement may consist in enduring his sufferings in the right way—an honorable way—in such a position man can, through loving contemplation of the image he carries of his beloved, achieve fulfillment. For the first time in my life I was able to understand the meaning of the words, "The angels are lost in perpetual contemplation of an infinite glory."

In front of me a man stumbled and those following him fell on top of him. The guard rushed over and used his whip on them all. Thus my thoughts were interrupted for a few minutes. But soon my soul found its way back from the prisoner's existence to another world, and I resumed talk with my loved one: I asked her questions, and she answered; she questioned me in return, and I answered.

"Stop!" We had arrived at our work site. Everybody rushed into the dark hut in the hope of getting a fairly decent tool. Each prisoner got a spade or a pickaxe.

"Can't you hurry up, you pigs?" Soon we had resumed the previous day's positions in the ditch. The frozen ground cracked under the point of the pickaxes, and sparks flew. The men were silent, their brains numb.

My mind still clung to the image of my wife. A thought crossed my mind: I didn't even know if she were still alive. I knew only one thing—which I have learned well by now: Love goes very far beyond the physical person of the beloved. It finds its deepest meaning in his spiritual being, his inner self. Whether or not he is actually present, whether or not he is still alive at all, ceases somehow to be of importance.

I did not know whether my wife was alive, and I had no means of finding out (during all my prison life there was no outgoing or incoming mail); but at that moment it ceased to matter. There was no need for me to know; nothing could touch the strength of my love, my thoughts, and the image of my beloved. Had I known then that my wife was dead, I think that I would still have given myself, undisturbed by that knowledge, to the contemplation of her image, and that my mental conversation with her would have been just as vivid and just as satisfying. "Set me like a seal upon thy heart, love is as strong as death."

The experiences of camp life show that man does have a choice of action. There were enough examples, often of a heroic nature, which proved that apathy could be overcome, irritability suppressed. Man *can* preserve a vestige of spiritual freedom, of independence of mind, even in such terrible conditions of psychic and physical stress.

We who lived in concentration camps can remember the men who walked through the huts comforting others, giving away their last piece of bread. They may have been few in number, but they offer sufficient proof that everything can be taken from a man but one thing: the last of the human freedoms—to choose one's attitude in any given set of circumstances, to choose one's own way.

And there were always choices to make. Every day, every hour, offered the opportunity to make a decision, a decision which determined whether you would or would not submit to those powers which threatened to rob you of your very self, your inner freedom; which determined whether or not you would become the plaything of circumstance, renouncing freedom and dignity to become molded into the form of the typical inmate.

The way in which a man accepts his fate and all the suffering it entails, the way in which he takes up his cross, gives him ample opportunity—even under the most difficult circumstances—to add a deeper meaning to his life. It may remain brave, dignified and unselfish. Or in the bitter fight for self-preservation he may forget his human dignity and become no more than an animal. Here lies the chance for a man either to make use of or to forgo the opportunities of attaining the moral values that a difficult situation may afford him. And this decides whether he is worthy of his sufferings or not.

Do not think that these considerations are unworldly and too far removed from real life. It is true that only a few people are capable of reaching such high moral standards. Of the prisoners only a few kept their full inner liberty and obtained those values which their suffering afforded, but even one such example is sufficient proof that man's inner strength may raise him above his outward fate. Such men are not only in concentration camps. Everywhere man is confronted with fate, with the chance of achieving something through his own suffering.

The Light of Stars
FROM *VOICES OF THE NIGHT*, 1839
By Henry Wadsworth Longfellow

The night is come, but not too soon;
And sinking silently,
All silently, the little moon
Drops down behind the sky.
There is no light in earth or heaven
But the cold light of stars;
And the first watch of night is given
To the red planet Mars.
Is it the tender star of love?

The star of love and dreams?

O no! from that blue tent above,

A hero's armor gleams.

And earnest thoughts within me rise,

When I behold afar,

Suspended in the evening skies,

The shield of that red star.

O star of strength! I see thee stand

And smile upon my pain;

Thou beckonest with thy mailed hand,

And I am strong again.

Within my breast there is no light

But the cold light of stars;

I give the first watch of the night

To the red planet Mars.

The star of the unconquered will,

He rises in my breast,

Serene, and resolute, and still,

And calm, and self-possessed.

And thou, too, whosoe'er thou art,

That readest this brief psalm,

As one by one thy hopes depart,

Be resolute and calm.

O fear not in a world like this,

And thou shalt know erelong,

Know how sublime a thing it is

To suffer and be strong.

CHAPTER FIVE
SELF-RELIANCE

The cowboy. The frontiersman. The pioneer.

These images of manliness still strongly resonate with Western men because they represent an ideal and virtue they often feel lacking in their own lives—that of self-reliance.

Our pioneer forefathers hewed a life for themselves out of the untamed soil with nothing but their wits and the sweat of their brow. They needed very little, and what they did need, they made. If it broke, they fixed it. Their nearest neighbors could be a few dozen miles away and solitude was simply a part of life.

Today we live in a time when almost everything a man does can be outsourced to someone else. Need your oil changed? Take it to a mechanic. Have a leaky roof? Call a repairman. Need food? Order take-out.

Even your thinking can be outsourced. A man's every musing can be posted on the Internet or texted to friends for immediate feedback. And answers to life's questions seem to be only a Google search away.

While modern conveniences and technology have happily freed us from much of the drudgery, danger, and hardship that our forebearers faced on the frontier, these advancements have also left many men feeling disconnected from their lives. They are plagued with a disconcerting sense of restlessness, feeling as if they are floating through life, that life is happening *to* them and being orchestrated by others.

Self-reliance is the antidote to this anxious drift. Seeking this virtue need not involve trading in your car for a covered wagon, donning buckskin pants, and retiring to a cave in the mountains. Or even erasing the pizza delivery man's number from your phone. Rather it's about coming to understand that while a boy depends on others for everything, a man is able to stand on his own two feet and make his own way. It's about fostering the confidence that even if the whole world went to pot around you, you'd still have the resources and inner fortitude to carry on. It's about cultivating the pioneering *spirit* and *attitude* at the core of your approach to life.

The self-reliant man doesn't wait around for his dreams to come true or for someone to fix his problems. He gets started right away and figures it out for himself as he goes.

The self-reliant man lives simply and frugally, without needing stuff to make him happy and avoiding the chains of debt.

The self-reliant man doesn't depend on others to validate his beliefs and decisions. He carves out his own path in life even if his ideas cut across the grain.

The self-reliant man enjoys associating with others, but can be perfectly content spending time in his own company.

In short, the self-reliant man enjoys supreme *freedom* and *independence* in all areas of his life. He is captain of his soul and master of his own destiny.

....

"Humility is the part of wisdom, and is most becoming in men. But let no one discourage self-reliance; it is, of all the rest, the greatest quality of true manliness." —Louis Kossuth

What Is Meant by Self-Reliance?
FROM *SELF-CULTURE & SELF-RELIANCE*, 1869
By William Unsworth

The questions are naturally suggested, "What kind of culture is intended? And what is meant by self-reliance?" … By self-culture is intended the cultivation of the powers and faculties nature has given you, and that to the greatest degree your opportunities and circumstances will allow: and this done by and for yourselves, with a view to improve your own condition here, as far as possible, and that you may stand on higher vantage-ground hereafter. And by self-reliance is meant a firm but modest dependence on your own capabilities, your own efforts and talents, in opposition to a weak and unmanly leaning upon foreign resources and assistance. These qualities blended and combined, will wonderfully help men through the world. But if they do not possess them in some tolerably good degree, they will be the football of their fellows, the sport of circumstances, and go down to death "sore sick at heart." They will be deeply mortified at their own fickleness, despised by others, and heartily despised by themselves.

"If you see anybody wail and complain, call him a slave, though he be clad in purple." —Epictetus

The Sturdiest Manhood
FROM THE SPEECH, "SELF-MADE MEN," 1859
By Frederick Douglass

. . . .

After escaping the shackles of slavery, Frederick Douglass (1818–1895) went on to become an author, newspaper publisher, and respected abolitionist. He was also a sought after and electrifying orator. During his life, "Self-Made Men" was his most popular speech. Having overcome the most oppressive of beginnings to achieve greatness, Douglass sincerely believed that such success was possible for any self-reliant man willing to put in the work.

. . . .

Self-made men are the men who, under peculiar difficulties and without the ordinary helps of favoring circumstances, have attained knowledge, usefulness, power and position and have learned from themselves the best uses to which life can be put in this world, and in the exercises of these uses to build up worthy character. They are the men who owe little or nothing to birth, relationship, or friendly surroundings; to wealth inherited or to early approved means of education; who are what they are, without the aid of any favoring conditions by which other men usually rise in the world and achieve great results. … They are in a peculiar sense indebted to themselves for themselves. If they have traveled far, they have made the road on which they have traveled. If they have ascended high, they have built their own ladder.

Though a man of this class need not claim to be a hero or to be worshiped as such, there is genuine heroism in his struggle and something of sublimity and glory in his triumph. Every instance of such success is an example and help to humanity. It, better than any mere assertion, gives us assurance of the latent powers and resources of simple and unaided manhood. It dignifies labor, honors application, lessens pain and depression, dispels gloom from the brow of the destitute and weariness from the heart of him about to faint, and enables man to take hold of the roughest and flintiest hardships incident to the battle of life, with a lighter heart, with higher hopes and a larger courage.

The various conditions of men and the different uses they make of their powers and opportunities in life, are full of puzzling contrasts and contradictions. Here, as elsewhere, it is easy to dogmatize, but it is not so easy to define, explain and demonstrate. The natural laws for the government, well-being and progress of mankind, seem to be equal and are equal; but the subjects of these laws everywhere abound in inequalities, discords, and contrast. We cannot have fruit without flowers, but we often have flowers without fruit. The promise of youth often breaks down in manhood, and real excellence often comes unheralded and from unexpected quarters.

The scene presented from this view is as a thousand arrows shot from the same point and aimed at the same object. United in aim, they are divided in flight. Some fly too high, others too low. Some go to the right, others to the left. Some fly too far, and others, not far enough, and only a few hit the mark. Such is life. United in the quiver, they are divided in the air. Matched when dormant, they are unmatched in action.

I do not think much of the good luck theory of self-made men. It is worth but little attention and has no practical value. An apple carelessly flung into a crowd may hit one person, or it may hit another, or it may hit nobody. The probabilities are precisely the same in this accident theory of self-made men. It divorces a man from his own achievements, contemplates him as a being of chance and leaves him without will, motive, ambition and aspiration. Yet the accident theory is among the most popular theories of individual success. It has about it the air of mystery which the multitudes so well like, and withal, it does something to mar the complacency of the successful.

It is one of the easiest and commonest things in the world for a successful man to be followed in his career through life and to have constantly pointed out this or that particular stroke of good fortune which fixed his destiny and made him successful. If not ourselves great, we like to explain why others are so. We are stingy in our praise to merit, but generous in our praise to chance. Besides, a man feels himself measurably great when he can point out the precise moment and circumstance which made his neighbor great. He easily fancies that the slight difference between himself and his friend is simply one of luck. It was his friend who was lucky, but it might easily have been himself. Then too, the next best thing to success is a valid apology for non-success. Detraction is, to many, a delicious morsel.

But the main objection to this very comfortable theory is that, like most other theories, it is made to explain too much. While it ascribes success to chance and friendly circumstances, it is apt to take no cognizance of the very different uses to which different men put their circumstances and their chances.

Fortune may crowd a man's life with fortunate circumstances and happy opportunities, but they will, as we all know, avail him nothing unless he makes a wise and vigorous use of them. It does not matter that the wind is fair and the tide at its flood, if the mariner refuses to weigh his anchor and spread his canvas to the breeze. The golden harvest is ripe in vain if the farmer refuses to reap. Opportunity is important but exertion is indispensable.

When we find a man who has ascended heights beyond ourselves; who has a broader range of vision than we and a sky with more stars in it than we have in ours, we may know that he has worked harder, better and more wisely than we. He was awake while we slept. He was busy while we were idle and was wisely improving his time and talents while we were wasting ours.

I am certain that there is nothing good, great or desirable which man can possess in this world, that does not come by some kind of labor of physical or mental, moral or spiritual. A man, at times, gets something for nothing, but it will, in his hands, amount to nothing. What is true in the world of matter, is equally true in the world of the mind. Without culture there can be no growth; without exertion, no acquisition; without friction, no polish; without labor, no knowledge; without action, no progress and without conflict, no victory. A man that lies down a fool at night, hoping that he will waken wise in the morning, will rise up in the morning as he laid down in the evening.

From these remarks it will be evident that, allowing only ordinary ability and opportunity, we may explain success mainly by one word and that word is WORK! WORK!! WORK!!! WORK!!!! Not transient and fitful effort, but patient, enduring, honest, unremitting and indefatigable work into which the whole heart is put, and which, in both temporal and spiritual affairs, is the true miracle worker. Everyone may avail himself of this marvelous power, if he will. There is no royal road to perfection. Certainly no one must wait for some kind of friend to put a springing board under his feet, upon which he may easily bound from the first round of their ladder onward and upward to its highest round. If he waits for this, he may wait long, and perhaps forever. He who does not think himself worth saving from poverty and ignorance by his own efforts, will hardly be thought worth the efforts of anybody else.

The lesson taught at this point by human experience is simply this, that the man who will get up will be helped up; and the man who will not get up will be allowed to stay down. This rule may appear somewhat harsh, but in its general application and operation it is wise, just and beneficent. I know of no other rule which can be substituted for it without bringing social chaos. Personal independence is a virtue and it is the soul out of which comes the sturdiest manhood. But there can be no independence without a large share of self-dependence, and this virtue cannot be bestowed. It must be developed from within.

Pioneers! O Pioneers!
FROM *LEAVES OF GRASS*, 1891
By Walt Whitman

Come my tan-faced children,
Follow well in order, get your weapons ready,
Have you your pistols? have you your sharp-edged axes?
Pioneers! O pioneers!

For we cannot tarry here,
We must march my darlings, we must bear the brunt of danger,

We the youthful sinewy races, all the rest on us depend,
Pioneers! O pioneers!

O you youths, Western youths,
So impatient, full of action, full of manly pride and friendship,
Plain I see you Western youths, see you tramping with the foremost,
Pioneers! O pioneers!

Have the elder races halted?
Do they droop and end their lesson, wearied over there beyond the seas?
We take up the task eternal, and the burden and the lesson,
Pioneers! O pioneers!

All the past we leave behind,
We debouch upon a newer mightier world, varied world,
Fresh and strong the world we seize, world of labor and the march,
Pioneers! O pioneers!

We detachments steady throwing,
Down the edges, through the passes, up the mountains steep,
Conquering, holding, daring, venturing as we
    go the unknown ways,
Pioneers! O pioneers!

We primeval forests felling,
We the rivers stemming,
    vexing we and piercing
    deep the mines within,
We the surface broad survey-
    ing, we the virgin soil
    upheaving,
Pioneers! O pioneers!

Colorado men are we,
From the peaks gigantic, from the great sierras and the high plateaus,
From the mine and from the gully, from the hunting trail we come,
Pioneers! O pioneers!

From Nebraska, from Arkansas,
Central inland race are we, from Missouri, with the continental
    blood intervein'd,
All the hands of comrades clasping, all the Southern, all the Northern,
Pioneers! O pioneers!

O resistless restless race!
O beloved race in all! O my breast aches with tender love for all!
O I mourn and yet exult, I am rapt with love for all,
Pioneers! O pioneers!

Raise the mighty mother mistress,
Waving high the delicate mistress, over all the starry mistress, (bend
    your heads all,)
Raise the fang'd and warlike mistress, stern, impassive, weapon'd mistress,
Pioneers! O pioneers!

See my children, resolute children,
By those swarms upon our rear we must never yield or falter,
Ages back in ghostly millions frowning there behind us urging,
Pioneers! O pioneers!

On and on the compact ranks,
With accessions ever waiting, with the places of the dead quickly fill'd,
Through the battle, through defeat, moving yet and never stopping,
Pioneers! O pioneers!

O to die advancing on!
Are there some of us to droop and die? has the hour come?

Then upon the march we fittest die, soon and sure the gap is fill'd.
Pioneers! O pioneers!

All the pulses of the world,
Falling in they beat for us, with the Western movement beat,
Holding single or together, steady moving to the front, all for us,
Pioneers! O pioneers!

Life's involv'd and varied pageants,
All the forms and shows, all the workmen at their work,
All the seamen and the landsmen, all the masters with their slaves,
Pioneers! O pioneers!

All the hapless silent lovers,
All the prisoners in the prisons, all the righteous and the wicked,
All the joyous, all the sorrowing, all the living, all the dying,
Pioneers! O pioneers!

I too with my soul and body,
We, a curious trio, picking, wandering on our way,
Through these shores amid the shadows, with the apparitions pressing,
Pioneers! O pioneers!

Lo, the darting bowling orb!
Lo, the brother orbs around, all the clustering suns and planets,
All the dazzling days, all the mystic nights with dreams,
Pioneers! O pioneers!

These are of us, they are with us,
All for primal needed work, while the followers there in embryo
     wait behind,
We to-day's procession heading, we the route for travel clearing,
Pioneers! O pioneers!

O you daughters of the West!
O you young and elder daughters! O you mothers and you wives!
Never must you be divided, in our ranks you move united,
Pioneers! O pioneers!

Minstrels latent on the prairies!
(Shrouded bards of other lands, you may rest, you have done your work,)
Soon I hear you coming warbling, soon you rise and tramp amid us,
Pioneers! O pioneers!

Not for delectations sweet,
Not the cushion and the slipper, not the peaceful and the studious,
Not the riches safe and palling, not for us the tame enjoyment,
Pioneers! O pioneers!

Do the feasters gluttonous feast?
Do the corpulent sleepers sleep? have they lock'd and bolted doors?
Still be ours the diet hard, and the blanket on the ground,
Pioneers! O pioneers!

Has the night descended?
Was the road of late so toilsome? did we stop
    discouraged nodding on our way?
Yet a passing hour I yield you in your
    tracks to pause oblivious,
Pioneers! O pioneers!

Till with sound of trumpet,
Far, far off the daybreak call—hark!
    how loud and clear I hear it wind,
Swift! to the head of the army!—
    swift! spring to your places,
Pioneers! O pioneers!

SELF-RELIANCE

> *"Men seem neither to understand their riches nor their strength; of the former they believe greater things than they should; of the latter much less. Self-reliance and self-denial will teach a man to drink out of his own cistern, and eat his own sweetbread, and to learn and labor truly to get his own living, and carefully to save and expend the good things committed to his trust."* —Francis Bacon

A Guarantee of Independence

FROM *THRIFT; OR, HOW TO GET ON IN THE WORLD*, 1881
By Samuel Smiles

As a guarantee of independence, the modest and plebeian quality of economy is at once ennobled and raised to the rank of one of the most meritorious of virtues. "Never treat money affairs with levity," said Bulwer; "money is character." Some of man's best qualities depend upon the right use of money—such as his generosity, benevolence, justice, honesty, and forethought. Many of his worst qualities also originate in the bad use of money— such as greed, miserliness, injustice, extravagance, and improvidence.

People who spend all that they earn are ever hanging on the brink of destitution. They must necessarily be weak and impotent—the slaves of time and circumstance. They keep themselves poor. They lose self-respect as well as the respect of others. It is impossible that they can be free and independent. To be thriftless is enough to deprive one of all manly spirit and virtue.

But a man with something saved, no matter how little, is in a different position. The little capital he has stored up is always a source of power. He is no longer the sport of time and fate. He can boldly look the world in the face. He is, in a manner, his own master. He can dictate his own terms. He can neither be bought nor sold. He can look forward with cheerfulness to an old age of comfort and happiness.

Interest Never Sleeps

FROM "THE SPECTER OF DEBT," 1938
By J. Reuben Clark Jr.

It is the rule of our financial and economic life in all the world that interest is to be paid on borrowed money. May I say something about interest?

Interest never sleeps nor sickens nor dies; it never goes to the hospital; it works on Sundays and holidays; it never takes a vacation; it never visits nor travels; it takes no pleasure; it is never laid off work nor discharged from employment; it never works on reduced hours ... Once in debt, interest is your companion every minute of the day and night; you cannot shun it or slip away from it; you cannot dismiss it; it yields neither to entreaties, demands, or orders; and whenever you get in its way or cross its course or fail to meet its demands, it crushes you.

"I have ever held it as a maxim never to do that through another which it was possible for me to execute myself." —Montesquieu

The Farmer and the Larks

Some larks had a nest in a field of grain. One evening the old larks coming home found the young ones in great terror. "We must leave our nest at once," they cried. Then they related how they had heard the farmer say that he must get his neighbors to come the next day and help him reap his field. "Oh," cried the old birds, "if that is all, we may rest quietly in our nest."

The next evening the young birds were found again in a state of terror. The farmer, it seems, was very angry because his neighbors had not come, and had said that he should get his relatives to come the next day to help him. The old birds took the news easily, and said there was nothing to fear yet.

SELF-RELIANCE

167

The next evening the young birds were quite cheerful. "Have you heard nothing today?" asked the old ones. "Nothing important," answered the young. "It is only that the farmer was angry because his relatives also failed him, and he said to his sons, 'Since neither our relatives nor our neighbors will help us, we must take hold tomorrow and do it ourselves.'"

The old birds were excited this time. They said, "We must leave our nest tonight. When a man decides to do a thing for himself, and to do it at once, you may be pretty sure that it will be done."

"For the man who makes everything that leads to happiness, or near to it, to depend upon himself, and not upon other men ... has adopted the very best plan for living happily. This is the man of moderation; this is the man of manly character and of wisdom." —Plato

The Frontiersman
FROM *SOULS-SPUR*, 1914
By Richard Wightman

The suns of summer seared his skin;
The cold his blood congealed;
The forest giants blocked his way
The stubborn acres' yield
He wrenched from them by dint of arm,
And grim old Solitude

Broke bread with him and shared his cot

Within the cabin rude.

The gray rocks gnarled his massive hands;

The north wind shook his frame;

The wolf of hunger bit him oft;

The world forgot his name;

But mid the lurch and crash of trees,

Within the clearing's span

Where now the bursting wheat-heads dip,

The fates turned out—a man!

"There is something captivating in spirit and intrepidity, to which we often yield, as to a resistless power; nor can he reasonably expect the confidence of others, who too apparently distrusts himself." —Samuel Johnson

Don't Be a Sheep; Be a Man
FROM *EDITORIALS FROM THE HEARST NEWSPAPERS*, 1906
By Arthur Brisbane

We inflict a piece of advice upon our readers. It is intended especially for the young, who have still to get their growth, whose characters and possibilities are forming.

Get away from the crowd when you can. Keep yourself to yourself, if only for a few hours daily.

Full individual growth, special development, rounded mental operations—all these demand room, separation from others, solitude, self-examination and the self-reliance which solitude gives.

The finest tree stands off by itself in the open plain. Its branches spread wide. It is a complete tree, better than the cramped tree in the crowded forest.

The animal to be admired is not that which runs in herds, the gentle browsing deer or foolish sheep thinking only as a fraction of the flock, incapable of personal independent direction. It's the lonely prowling lion or the big black leopard with the whole world for his private field that is worth looking at.

The man who grows up in a herd, deer-like, thinking with the herd, acting with the herd, rarely amounts to anything.

Do you want to succeed? Grow in solitude, work, develop in solitude, with books and thoughts and nature for friends. Then, if you want the crowd to see how fine you are, come back to it and boss it if it will let you.

Here is what Goethe says: "Es bildet ein Talent sich in der Stille, doch ein Charakter in dem Strome der Welt." (Talent is developed in solitude, character in the rush of the world.)

Don't be a sheep or a deer. Don't devote your hours to the company and conversation of those who know as little as you do. Don't think hard only when you are trying to remember a popular song or to decide on the color of your winter overcoat or necktie.

Remember that you are an individual, not a grain of dust or a blade of grass. Don't be a sheep; be a man. It has taken nature a hundred million years to produce you. Don't make her sorry she took the time.

Get out in the park and walk and think. Get up in your hall bedroom, read, study, write what you think. Talk more to yourself and less to others. Avoid magazines, avoid excessive newspaper reading.

There is not a man of average ability but could make a striking career if he could but *will* to do the best that is in him.

Proofs of growth due to solitude are endless. Milton's greatest work was done when blindness, old age and the death of the Puritan government forced him into completest seclusion. Beethoven did his best work in the solitude of deafness.

Bacon would never have been the great leader of scientific thought had not his trial and disgrace forced him from the company of a grand retinue and stupid court to the solitude of his own brain.

"Multum insola fuit anima mea." (My spirit hath been much alone.) This he said often, and lucky it was for him. Loneliness of spirit made him.

Get a little of it for yourself.

Drop your club, your street corner, your gossipy boarding-house table. Drop your sheep life and try being a man.

It may improve you.

Always Try It Yourself

FROM *ETHICS FOR YOUNG PEOPLE*, 1891
By Charles Carroll Everett

It is important to learn early to rely upon yourself; for little has been done in the world by those who are always looking out for some one to help them.

We must be on our guard not to confound self-reliance with self-conceit, yet the difference between the two cannot easily be defined in words. The difference is something like that between bravery and foolhardiness. The self-conceited person takes it for granted that he is superior to others. Self-reliance is very different from this. The self-reliant person is often very modest. He does not say about anything that is to be done, "I am so strong and wise that I can do it." He says, "I will try, and if patience and hard work will do it, it shall be done."

One way in which a person may become self-reliant, is never to seek or accept help till he has fairly tried what can be done without it.

Some scholars, if they come to a problem that seems hard, run at once to the teacher, or an older friend, or perhaps even to another scholar, who is brighter or more self-reliant than themselves, in order to be told how to do it. Always try it yourself. Even if it is nothing more important than a conundrum, do not wish somebody to tell you the answer till you have fairly tried to conquer it.

It is a pleasant feeling that comes from having done a difficult thing one's self, a feeling that those never have who are helped out of every hard place.

Did you ever think why it is that so many of the great men of our country are found among those who began life in hardship and poverty? Many of them grew up in what was, when they were young, the western frontier, where they had to work hard; where they had no schools, and few comforts and conveniences. They have come from these circumstances that seemed so discouraging, and have become presidents, judges, generals, or millionaires.

One reason why so many that had such an unpromising beginning have won such success is that because they had so few helps, they were forced

CHAPTER FIVE

to help themselves. They thus became self-reliant. When they went out into the world they went straight ahead. Without waiting for any one to make a place for them, they made a place for themselves. Without waiting for any one to do for them, they did for themselves. Without waiting for people to advise them they trusted themselves. They were prompt, energetic and sensible. Thus people trusted them and honored them.

Though you have the helps that such men were forced to do without, yet you can cultivate the habit of self-reliance. You can solve your own problems, do your own tasks, and meet your own difficulties; and thus you, too, can be preparing to do your own part in the world.

"I was the first to step out freely along a hitherto untravelled route; I have not trod in the footsteps of others: he who relies on himself is the leader to guide the swarm." —Horace

Our Job Was to Do Whatever We Could Do

FROM *WE WHO ARE ALIVE AND REMAIN:*
UNTOLD STORIES FROM THE BAND OF BROTHERS, 2009
By Marcus Brotherton

Historian Stephen Ambrose believed that a key to Allied success in World War II was the ability of American soldiers to think as individuals. While the Japanese and German soldiers were highly trained and zealously devoted, when their line of command broke down, the men were left not knowing how to proceed. The American soldiers, in contrast, were able to think creatively and take initiative in the absence of direct orders. This was exemplified on D-Day when Easy Company's paratroopers were dropped far from their intended targets and scattered from each other. Instead of being paralyzed by indecision, the men banded together whomever they could find, and as individuals and little groups did whatever they could to further the mission as they tried to find their companies.

Some, like Ed Pepping, never made it back to their men, but got to work in whatever situation they found themselves and in whatever capacity they could.

. . . .

ED PEPPING

We were dropped much lower and faster than anticipated. On the way down I remember seeing burn holes in my parachute from the bullets going through. I came in backward and landed in the middle of a field. I didn't have enough time to pull up on the risers and alleviate the shock of landing. The back of my helmet hit the back of my head. I didn't know it at the time but I had cracked three vertebrate and received a concussion. All I knew was that I kept blacking out and coming to. That blacking in and out happened all the time I was there. I have a lot of blank spots in my memory of Normandy. I can remember only about half the time I was there. It comes in bits and pieces.

When I landed, I had nothing except a knife. As a medic I never carried a rifle anyway, but the speed of the jump and the opening shock had ripped all my medical equipment off me. That was very frustrating. It had taken weeks to pack the equipment, but the frustrating part was that I had nothing to work with. You can imagine, a lot of the wounds seen were catastrophic.

As medics, our job was to do whatever we could do. On the first day I was on the way to join the guys and was called into a building being used as an aid station. We had no evac at the time. A guy had a big sucking chest wound, a wound they had only told us about but never seen firsthand. The only thing I could do was close the wound up as best I could. I couldn't stay there to see that he was evacuated. I don't know if the man lived or not. That was the way it was. Time after time we saw guys lose legs and arms, chest wounds, guys all shot up and bloody. A man can bleed to death in a couple of minutes. If it hadn't been for the wonderful doctors we had—the guys who had some serious medical experience—we would have lost so many more men.

You have to realize that a medic is no doctor. Our job was to reach a wounded man as quickly as possible out on the field, get him stabilized by bandaging and giving him morphine, then get him back to a doctor—if you could. But if you don't have any bandages or morphine, what can you do? You scrounge around and find whatever you can. When you come across catastrophic wounds—what can a medic ever do about those? It's not like I had a first-aid book with me or could call up a doctor on the phone.

That same day, the first day, I went to a church in Angoville au Plein that was being used as an aid station. One of our guys had found an abandoned German jeep somewhere and was bringing in as many casualties as he could. I helped him out for quite a while. The people in that church have never taken the blood stains off those pews. They contacted me a few years back to ask me if I wanted my name put on a memorial there. I said, "Heck no. All I did was bring people in."

Outside Beaumont, there was a lot of fire going on. Lieutenant Colonel Billy Turner, 1st Battalion's commanding officer, stood on top of a tank turret and directed fire at a .75. He was hit in the head by a sniper's bullet and collapsed. Since he was at the front of a six-tank column, the whole advance halted, exposing the column to enemy fire. I ran over and leaned headfirst into the tank's turret where he had fallen. With the help of the tank's crew I pulled the battalion commander out just before he died. It was an agonizing moment. Lieutenant Colonel Turner was a good man and much revered. At least the tank column could keep moving again.

I never did get back to my unit. The last thing I remember was being in Carentan with three others, walking headlong through town in an attempt to reach E Company. All I knew was that they were meeting fierce resistance and needed medics. The next thing I knew, I was in the hospital with a cast on my leg from ankle to hip. I have no idea why. I have no recollection of how I got wounded. There was no record of anybody picking me up. One moment I was trying to get back to my unit. The next minute I was in the hospital cast.

In the hospital I got the Purple Heart, the Bronze Star for my action trying to save Lieutenant Colonel Turner (I never knew who recommended me for it), and the Croix de Guerre. Somebody stole my uniform, all my equipment, my medals, and everything I had.

They wouldn't send me back to my unit because of my condition. They figured that because I was still in and out I either had a concussion or was a victim of combat fatigue. They ran me through all these tests. A doctor determined I had a severe concussion and had cracked three vertebrate in my neck. Those were causing the blackouts.

That was all I needed to know. Five of us decided to go AWOL, left the hospital, and went back to the 506th. I was with the unit for fifty-one days trying to get set up to go to Holland. It's funny—for those fifty-one days I'm still counted AWOL, even though I was back with my unit. After that time they sent me to the general hospital in England to serve in the seriously wounded ward. I was still blacking out occasionally.

Working in the ward turned out to be one of my favorite experiences. Sometimes we worked two or three days straight on the guys, if a convoy came in, but it felt like we could actually do some good for the men. The doctors and nurses took me under their wing. I got so I could give penicillin shots without waking a guy up. That felt important. It was an honor to serve in that ward.

It's true, we saw some horrific things in the ward. Some guys were in really bad shape. The Germans had a land mine called the castrator. It was a long bullet about eight inches long. They stuck it in the soil, and all that could be seen was the tip of the bullet. Guys stepped on it, and the blast went up the leg. One night we had thirty-four men wounded in this manner. Some lost legs, some had their lower legs shattered. You can imagine it.

I stayed with the general hospital in England until I was transferred to another general hospital, in France. There, I helped the chaplain. When I was a kid, I had found out that I was immune to almost all the common diseases. So the chaplain had me go into the communicable-disease ward to talk to the guys.

After that I operated a switchboard for trunk lines throughout France. I don't know how I got hooked up with that, but I took to it naturally.

Man Is Strong Only as He Is Strong From Within

FROM *SELF-CONTROL, ITS KINGSHIP AND MAJESTY*, 1905
By William George Jordan

Self-confidence without self-reliance, is as useless as a cooking recipe— without food. Self-confidence sees the possibilities of the individual; self-reliance realizes them.

The man who is self-reliant says ever: "No one can realize my possibilities for me, but me; no one can make me good or evil but myself." He works out his own salvation—financially, socially, mentally, physically, and morally.

All the athletic exercises in the world are of no value to the individual unless he compel those bars and dumbbells to yield to him, in strength and muscle, the power for which he, himself, pays in time and effort. He can never develop his muscles by sending his valet to a gymnasium.

All that others can do for us is to give us opportunity. We must ever be prepared for the opportunity when it comes, and to go after it and find it when it does not come, or that opportunity is to us—nothing. Life is but a succession of opportunities. They are for good or evil—as we make them.

Many of the alchemists of old felt that they lacked but one element; if they could obtain that one, they believed they could transmute the baser metals into pure gold. It is so in character. There are individuals with rare mental gifts, and delicate spiritual discernment who fail utterly in life because they lack the one element—self-reliance. This would unite all their energies, and focus them into strength and power.

The man who is not self-reliant is weak, hesitating and doubting in all he does. He fears to take a decisive step, because he dreads failure, because he is waiting for someone to advise him or because he dare not act in accordance with his own best judgment. In his cowardice and his conceit he sees all his non-success due to others. He is "not appreciated," "not recognized," he is "kept down." He feels that in some subtle way "society is conspiring against him." He grows almost vain as he thinks that no one has had such poverty, such sorrow, such affliction, such failure as have come to him.

The man who is self-reliant seeks ever to discover and conquer the weakness within him that keeps him from the attainment of what he holds dearest; he seeks within himself the power to battle against all outside influences. He realizes that all the greatest men in history, in every phase of human effort, have been those who have had to fight against the odds of sickness, suffering, sorrow. To him, defeat is no more than passing through a tunnel is to a traveller—he knows he must emerge again into the sunlight.

The nation that is strongest is the one that is most self-reliant, the one that contains within its boundaries all that its people need. If, with its ports all blockaded it has not within itself the necessities of life and the elements of its continual progress then—it is weak, held by the enemy, and it is but a question of time till it must surrender. Its independence is in proportion to its self-reliance, to its power to sustain itself from within. What is true of nations is true of individuals. The history of nations is but the biography of individuals magnified, intensified, multiplied, and projected on the screen of the past. History is the biography of a nation; biography is the history of an individual. So it must be that the individual who is most strong in any trial, sorrow or need is he who can live from his inherent strength, who needs no scaffolding of commonplace sympathy to uphold him. He must ever be self-reliant.

The wealth and prosperity of ancient Rome, relying on her slaves to do the real work of the nation, proved the nation's downfall. The constant dependence on the captives of war to do the thousand details of life for them, killed self-reliance in the nation and in the individual. Then, through weakened self-reliance and the increased opportunity for idle, luxurious

CHAPTER FIVE

ease that came with it, Rome, a nation
of fighters, became a nation of men
more effeminate than women. As we
depend on others to do those things
we should do ourselves, our self-reliance weakens and our powers and
our control of them becomes con-
tinuously less.

Man to be great must be self-
reliant. Though he may not be so in
all things, he must be self-reliant in the
one in which he would be great. This
self-reliance is not the self-sufficien-
cy of conceit. It is daring to stand
alone. Be an oak, not a vine.

Be ready to give support, but do
not crave it; do not be dependent on it.
To develop your true self-reliance, you must see from the very beginning
that life is a battle you must fight for yourself—you must be your own
soldier. You cannot buy a substitute, you cannot win a reprieve, you can
never be placed on the retired list. The retired list of life is—death. The
world is busy with its own cares, sorrows and joys, and pays little heed to
you. There is but one great password to success—self-reliance.

If you would learn to converse, put yourself into positions where you
must speak. If you would conquer your morbidness, mingle with the bright
people around you, no matter how difficult it may be. If you desire the
power that someone else possesses, do not envy his strength, and dissipate
your energy by weakly wishing his force were yours. Emulate the process
by which it became his, depend on your self-reliance, pay the price for it,
and equal power may be yours. The individual must look upon himself as
an investment of untold possibilities if rightly developed—a mine whose

resources can never be known but by going down into it and bringing out what is hidden.

Man can develop his self-reliance by seeking constantly to surpass himself. We try too much to surpass others. If we seek ever to surpass ourselves, we are moving on a uniform line of progress, that gives a harmonious unifying to our growth in all its parts. Daniel Morrell, at one time President of the Cambria Rail Works, that employed 7,000 men and made a rail famed throughout the world, was asked the secret of the great success of the works. "We have no secret," he said, "but this—we always try to beat our last batch of rails." Competition is good, but it has its danger side. There is a tendency to sacrifice real worth to mere appearance, to have seeming rather than reality. But the true competition is the competition of the individual with himself—his present seeking to excel his past. This means real growth from within. Self-reliance develops it, and it develops self-reliance. Let the individual feel thus as to his own progress and possibilities, and he can almost create his life as he will. Let him never fall down in despair at dangers and sorrows at a distance; they may be harmless, like Bunyan's stone lions, when he nears them.

The man who is self-reliant does not live in the shadow of someone else's greatness; he thinks for himself, depends on himself, and acts for himself. In throwing the individual thus back upon himself it is not shutting his eyes to the stimulus and light and new life that come with the warm pressure of the hand, the kindly word and sincere expressions of true friendship. But true friendship is rare; its great value is in a crisis—like a lifeboat. Many a boasted friend has proved a leaking, worthless "lifeboat" when the storm of adversity might make him useful. In these great crises of life, man is strong only as he is strong from within, and the more he depends on himself the stronger will he become, and the more able will he be to help others in the hour of their need. His very life will be a constant help and a strength to others, as he becomes to them a living lesson of the dignity of self-reliance.

Hercules and the Wagoner
An Aesop's Fable

As a Wagoner drove his wagon through a miry lane, the wheels stuck fast in the clay, so that the horses could proceed no further. The man, without making the least effort to remedy the matter, fell upon his knees, and began to call upon Hercules to come and help him out of his trouble.

"Lazy fellow," said Hercules, "lay your own shoulder to the wheel. Stir yourself, and do what you can. Then, if you want aid from me, you shall have it."

Heaven helps those who help themselves.

> *"Do what thy manhood bids thee do*
> *from none but self expect applause;*
> *He noblest lives and noblest dies*
> *who makes and keeps his self-made laws."*
> —*Richard Francis Burton*

Whoso Would Be a Man Must Be a Nonconformist

FROM THE ESSAY "SELF-RELIANCE," IN *ESSAYS, FIRST SERIES*, 1841
By Ralph Waldo Emerson

I read the other day some verses written by an eminent painter which were original and not conventional. The soul always hears an admonition in such lines, let the subject be what it may. The sentiment they instil is of more value than any thought they may contain. To believe your own thought, to believe that what is true for you in your private heart is true for all men—that is genius. Speak your latent conviction, and it shall be the universal sense; for the inmost in due time becomes the outmost—and our first thought is rendered back to us by the trumpets of the Last Judgment. Familiar as the voice of the mind is to each, the highest merit we ascribe to Moses, Plato, and Milton is, that they set at naught books and traditions, and spoke not what men but what they thought. A man should learn to detect and watch that gleam of light which flashes across his mind from within, more than the lustre of the firmament of bards and sages. Yet he dismisses without notice his thought, because it is his. In every work of genius we recognize our own rejected thoughts: they come back to us with a certain alienated majesty. Great works of art have no more affecting lesson for us than this. They teach us to abide by our spontaneous impression with good-humored inflexibility then most when the whole cry of voices is on the other side. Else, to-morrow a stranger will say with masterly good sense precisely what we have thought and felt all the time, and we shall be forced to take with shame our own opinion from another.

Trust thyself: every heart vibrates to that iron string. Accept the place the divine providence has found for you, the society of your contemporaries, the connection of events. Great men have always done so, and confided themselves childlike to the genius of their age, betraying their perception that the absolutely trustworthy was seated at their heart, working through their hands, predominating in all their being. And we are now men, and must accept in the highest mind the same transcendent destiny; and not minors and invalids in a protected corner, not cowards fleeing before a revolution, but guides, redeemers, and benefactors, obeying the Almighty effort, and advancing on Chaos and the Dark.

Society everywhere is in conspiracy against the manhood of every one of its members. Society is a joint-stock company, in which the members agree, for the better securing of his bread to each shareholder, to surrender the liberty and culture of the eater. The virtue in most request is conformity. Self-reliance is its aversion. It loves not realities and creators, but names and customs.

Whoso would be a man must be a nonconformist. He who would gather immortal palms must not be hindered by the name of goodness, but must explore if it be goodness. Nothing is at last sacred but the integrity of your own mind. Absolve you to yourself, and you shall have the suffrage of the world.

What I must do is all that concerns me, not what the people think. This rule, equally arduous in actual and in intellectual life, may serve for the whole distinction between greatness and meanness. It is the harder, because you will always find those who think they know what is your duty better than you know it. It is easy in the world to live after the world's opinion; it is easy in solitude to live after our own; but the great man is he who in the midst of the crowd keeps with perfect sweetness the independence of solitude.

"Self-reliance is a noble and manly quality of the character; and he who exercises it in small matters schools himself by that discipline for its exercise in matters of more momentous importance, and for exigencies when the help of others— readily proffered in ordinary cases—may not be offered, or, if offered, may be unavailing for his aid in the emergency."
—The Christian Globe

Every Man Should Be Able to Save His Own Life

FROM *ENDURANCE*, 1926
By Earle Liederman

Every man should be able to save his own life. He should be able to swim far enough, run fast and long enough to save his life in case of emergency and necessity. He also should be able to chin himself a reasonable number of times, as well as to dip a number of times, and he should be able to jump a reasonable height and distance.

If he is of the fat, porpoise type, naturally he cannot do all, if any, of these things; he has nobody to blame but himself, and his way of living that has brought his body into its condition of obesity.

Suppose—and it has happened many times—there should be a fire at sea or on lake or river; should one be half a mile or more from the shore, he would be mighty thankful to realize, were he compelled to jump for his life from the fire, that he could swim that distance and reach the shore in safety.

Suppose one were in a burning building and he had to lower himself hand under hand down a rope or down an improvised rope of bedclothing tied together to reach the ground in safety; he again would be thankful a thousand times that he possessed the strength and endurance in his arms and coordinate muscles that would enable him to save himself. Such things never may happen, and let us hope they do not, but what has happened always is possible to occur again—and, in fact, always is happening to someone.

I do not believe in everyone striving to be a long distance swimmer, a long distance runner, or any kind of endurance athlete.

But he should be able to swim at least half a mile or more; he should be able to run at top speed two hundred yards or more; he should be able to jump over obstacles higher than his waist; and he should be in condition to pull his body upward by the strength of his arms, until his chin touches his hands, at least fifteen to twenty times; and as for pushing ability, he should be able to dip between parallel bars or between two chairs at least twenty-five times or more.

If he can accomplish these things he need have no fear concerning the safety of his life should he be forced into an emergency from which he alone may be able to save himself.

"I was taught to endure labor, to want little, and to do things myself." —*Marcus Aurelius*

Simplify, Simplify
FROM *WALDEN*, 1854
By Henry David Thoreau

I went to the woods because I wished to live deliberately, to front only the essential facts of life, and see if I could not learn what it had to teach, and not, when I came to die, discover that I had not lived. I did not wish to live what was not life, living is so dear; nor did I wish to practise resignation, unless it was quite necessary. I wanted to live deep and suck out all the marrow of life, to live so sturdily and Spartan-like as to put to rout all that was not life, to cut a broad swath and shave close, to drive life into a corner, and reduce it to its lowest terms, and, if it proved to be mean, why then to get the whole and genuine meanness of it, and publish its meanness to the world; or if it were sublime, to know it by experience, and be able

to give a true account of it in my next excursion. For most men, it appears to me, are in a strange uncertainty about it, whether it is of the devil or of God, and have *somewhat hastily* concluded that it is the chief end of man here to "glorify God and enjoy him forever."

Still we live meanly, like ants; though the fable tells us that we were long ago changed into men; like pygmies we fight with cranes; it is error upon error, and clout upon clout, and our best virtue has for its occasion a superfluous and evitable wretchedness. Our life is frittered away by detail. An honest man has hardly need to count more than his ten fingers, or in extreme cases he may add his ten toes, and lump the rest. Simplicity, simplicity, simplicity! I say, let your affairs be as two or three, and not a hundred or a thousand; instead of a million count half a dozen, and keep your accounts on your thumb-nail. In the midst of this chopping sea of civilized life, such are the clouds and storms and quicksands and thousand-and-one items to be allowed for, that a man has to live, if he would not founder and go to the bottom and not make his port at all, by dead reckoning, and he must be a great calculator indeed who succeeds. Simplify, simplify.

CHAPTER SIX
DISCIPLINE

Every man has a latent power within him. Author Sam Keen called this energy our "fire in the belly." Plato called it *thumos*, or manly spiritedness. Thumos is a man's life force, the engine of soul which inspires bold, courageous action and the pursuit of glory.

Plato believed that thumos was just one of the three parts of a man's psyche, the other two being his reason and his appetites. In the *Phaedrus*, Plato used the symbol of a chariot to explain the interplay of forces in this tripartite view of the soul. The chariot is pulled by two winged horses, one white, the other dark. The white horse, willing, strong, and handsome, represents a man's thumos, or noble ambition. The dark horse, obstinate, lumbering, and deformed, represents man's bodily appetites. Guiding these horses is the Charioteer, symbolizing reason and intellect. Reason is tasked with guiding and disciplining the two disparate steeds. When the white horse is directed towards honorable aims, it serves as the ally of the Charioteer. Together they force the stubborn black horse to fall into line and pull the chariot into the heavens. Without Reason holding tightly the reins, the two horses would move in opposite directions or not at all. In other words, harnessing one's passions through *discipline* is the only way for a man to move forward in life and reach his full potential.

Discipline. It's not a very popular word these days. It may bring to mind punishment—getting disciplined by one's parents or teachers. And in a culture that venerates instant gratification, quick fixes, and a "do whatever you *feel* like" attitude, discipline is often seen as constraining and cruel. But the truest discipline comes from within and is a man's chief source of power. While it may seem like a paradox, only by placing constraints and limits on ourselves can we truly become free and thus progress as men.

Many young men today grow up thinking that greatness can come without sacrifice and discipline. They want an impressive physique without having to dedicate hours to disciplined diet and exercise. They want to amass riches without having to discipline themselves with a monthly budget. They want stellar grades without disciplined, focused study. But as several selections in this book proclaim, "There is no royal road to success!" Discipline is the price we must pay to obtain our deepest desires and become our best selves.

When you take a step back, discipline is the linchpin virtue that makes acquiring the other manly virtues possible. Developing courage requires a man to have the discipline to step outside his comfort zone on a regular basis. Becoming industrious requires the discipline to get up and work, even when your mind and body tell you to stay on the couch. Developing the virtue of resolution requires the mental and sometimes physical discipline needed to keep going despite the overwhelming odds against you.

Our goal as men should be to become like the Charioteer in Plato's allegory: reining in our appetites, guiding our spiritedness, and disciplining ourselves on the path to godlike greatness.

The selections in this chapter, while thoroughly engaging and insightful, are longer and meatier than the rest. This is by design; reading them is an excellent first step in developing your discipline!

A King or a Slave
FROM *SELF-CONTROL, ITS KINGSHIP AND MAJESTY*, 1905
By William George Jordan

Every step in the progress of the world has been a new "control." It has been escaping from the tyranny of a fact, to the understanding and mastery of that fact. For ages man looked in terror at the lightning flash; today he has begun to understand it as electricity, a force he has mastered and made his slave. The million phases of electrical invention are but manifestations of our control over a great force. But the greatest of all "control" is self-control.

At each moment of man's life he is either a King or a slave. As he surrenders to a wrong appetite, to any human weakness; as he falls prostrate in hopeless subjection to any condition, to any environment, to any failure, he is a slave. As he day by day crushes out human weakness, masters opposing elements within him, and day by day re-creates a new self from the sin and folly of his past—then he is a King. He is a King ruling with wisdom over himself. Alexander conquered the whole world except—Alexander. Emperor of the earth, he was the servile slave of his own passions.

Any man may attain self-control if he only will. He must not expect to gain it save by long continued payment of price, in small progressive expenditures of energy. Nature is a thorough believer in the installment plan in her relations with the individual. No man is so poor that he cannot *begin* to pay for what he wants, and every small, individual payment that he makes, Nature stores and accumulates for him as a reserve fund in his hour of need.

With Nature, the mental, the physical or the moral energy he expends daily in right doing is all stored for him and transmuted into strength.

It is only the progressive installment plan Nature recognizes. No man can make a habit in a moment or break it in a moment. It is a matter of development, of growth. But at any moment man may *begin* to make or begin to break any habit.

This view of the growth of character should be a mighty stimulus to the man who sincerely desires and determines to live nearer to the limit of his possibilities.

Self-control may be developed in precisely the same manner as we tone up a weak muscle—by little exercises day by day. Let us each day do, as mere exercises of discipline in moral gymnastics, a few acts that are disagreeable to us, the doing of which will help us in instant action in our hour of need. The exercises may be very simple—dropping for a time an intensely interesting book at the most thrilling page of the story; jumping out of bed at the first moment of waking; walking home when one is perfectly able to do so, but when the temptation is to take a car; talking to some disagreeable person and trying to make the conversation pleasant. These daily exercises in moral discipline will have a wondrous tonic effect on man's whole moral nature.

The individual can attain self-control in great things only through self-control in little things. He must study himself to discover what is the weak point in his armor, what is the element within him that ever keeps him from his fullest success. This is the characteristic upon which he should begin his exercise in self-control. Is it selfishness, vanity, cowardice, morbidness, temper, laziness, worry, mind-wandering, lack of purpose?—whatever form human weakness assumes in the masquerade of life he must discover. He must then live each day as if his whole existence were telescoped down to the single day before him. With no useless regret for the past, no useless worry for the future, he should live that day as if it were his only day—the only day left for him to assert all that is best in him, the only day left for him to conquer all that is worst in him. He should master the weak element within him at each slight manifestation from moment to moment. Each moment then must be a victory for it or for him. Will he be King, or will he be slave?—the answer rests with him.

> *"No steam or gas ever drives anything until it is confined. No Niagara is ever turned into light and power until it is tunneled. No life ever grows until it is focused, dedicated, disciplined."* —Harry Emerson Fosdick

Discipline: The Means to an End

FROM *SELF-KNOWLEDGE AND SELF-DISCIPLINE*, 1916
By Basil William Maturin

We do not endure [self-discipline] merely for its own sake, but for what lies beyond it. And we bear those acts of self-denial and self-restraint because we feel and know full well that through such acts alone can we regain the mastery over all our misused powers and learn to use them with a vigour and a joy such as we have never known before.

It is as though one who had a great talent for music but had no technical training, and consequently could never produce the best results of his art, were to put himself under a great master. The first lessons he will have to learn will be, for the most part, to correct his mistakes, not to do this and not to do that; it will seem to him that he has lost all his former freedom of expression, that he is held back by all sorts of technical rules, that whenever he seeks to let himself go he is checked and hampered. And it is no doubt true. But he will soon begin to realise that as he learns more and suffers in the learning, possibilities of utterance reveal themselves which he has never dreamed of. He knows, he feels, that he is on the right path, and as the channels are prepared and the barriers against the old bad methods more firmly fixed, he feels the mighty tide of his genius rise and swell, he hears the shout of the gathering waters as they sweep before them every obstacle and pour forth in a mad torrent of glorious sound. All those days of restraint and suffering are crowned with the joy of the full and perfect expression of his art. The restraint and discipline he knew full well in those seemingly unfruitful days were but the means to an end. The end is always before him, and the end is positive expression. The dying to his old untrained and bad methods is but the birth throes of a larger and richer action.

"Not being able to govern events, I govern myself."
—Michel de Montaigne

Virtue Is a Mean
From *Nicomachean Ethics*, c. 350 B.C.
By Aristotle

Virtue, then, being of two kinds, intellectual and moral, intellectual virtue in the main owes both its birth and its growth to teaching (for which reason it requires experience and time), while moral virtue comes about as a result of habit, whence also its name (*ethike*) is one that is formed by a slight variation from the word *ethos* (habit). From this it is also plain that none of the moral virtues arises in us by nature; for nothing that exists by nature can form a habit contrary to its nature. For instance the stone which by nature moves downwards cannot be habituated to move upwards, not even if one tries to train it by throwing it up ten thousand times; nor can fire be habituated to move downwards, nor can anything else that by nature behaves in one way be trained to behave in another. Neither by nature, then, nor contrary to nature do the virtues arise in us; rather we are adapted by nature to receive them, and are made perfect by habit.

The virtues we get by first exercising them, as also happens in the case of the arts as well. For the things we have to learn before we can do them, we learn by doing them, e.g., men become builders by building and lyreplayers by playing the lyre; so too we become just by doing just acts, temperate by doing temperate acts, brave by doing brave acts.

Again, it is from the same causes and by the same means that every virtue is both produced and destroyed, and

similarly every art; for it is from playing the lyre that both good and bad lyreplayers are produced. And the corresponding statement is true of builders and of all the rest; men will be good or bad builders as a result of building well or badly. For if this were not so, there would have been no need of a teacher, but all men would have been born good or bad at their craft. This, then, is the case with the virtues also; by doing the acts that we do in our transactions with other men we become just or unjust, and by doing the acts that we do in the presence of danger, and being habituated to feel fear or confidence, we become brave or cowardly. The same is true of appetites and feelings of anger; some men become temperate and good-tempered, others self-indulgent and irascible, by behaving in one way or the other in the appropriate circumstances. Thus, in one word, states of character arise out of like activities. This is why the activities we exhibit must be of a certain kind; it is because the states of character correspond to the differences between these. It makes no small difference, then,

whether we form habits of one kind or of another from our very youth; it makes a very great difference, or rather all the difference.

First, then, let us consider this, that it is the nature of such things to be destroyed by defect and excess, as we see in the case of strength and of health (for to gain light on things imperceptible we must use the evidence of sensible things); both excessive and defective exercise destroys the strength, and similarly drink or food which is above or below a certain amount destroys the health, while that which is proportionate both produces and increases and preserves it. So too is it, then, in the case of temperance and courage and the other virtues. For the man who flies from and fears everything and does not stand his ground against anything becomes a coward, and the man who fears nothing at all but goes to meet every danger becomes rash; and similarly the man who indulges in every pleasure and abstains from none becomes self-indulgent, while the man who shuns every pleasure, as boors do, becomes in a way insensible; temperance and courage, then, are destroyed by excess and defect, and preserved by the mean.

Virtue, then, is a state of character concerned with choice, lying in a mean, i.e. the mean relative to us, this being determined by a rational principle, and by that principle by which the man of practical wisdom would determine it. Now it is a mean between two vices, that which depends on excess and that which depends on defect; and again it is a mean because the vices respectively fall short of or exceed what is right in both passions and actions, while virtue both finds and chooses that which is intermediate. Hence in respect of its substance and the definition which states its essence virtue is a mean, with regard to what is best and right an extreme.

Hence ... it is no easy task to be good. For in everything it is no easy task to find the middle, e.g., to find the middle of a circle is not for every one but for him who knows; so, too, any one can get angry—that is easy—or give or spend money; but to do this to the right person, to the right extent, at the right time, with the right motive, and in the right way, that is not for every one, nor is it easy; wherefore goodness is both rare and laudable and noble.

"First we make our habits, then our habits make us." —John Dryden

The Force of Habit

FROM *ETHICS FOR YOUNG PEOPLE*, 1891
By Charles Carroll Everett

In speaking of the influence of companions, I said that a man tends to imitate the persons by whom he is surrounded; and we saw that while this tendency may work harm, it may also work much good: and that in fact the development of civilization has been largely dependent upon this tendency.

Most of all, *a man tends to imitate himself.* The fact that he has done a thing once, in a certain way, makes it easier for him to do it again in the same way. The oftener this is repeated, the more fixed does the habit become. At last he cannot do the thing in a different way without great effort. Finally it may become almost impossible for him to do it in a different way.

It is interesting to see the force of habit in little things. In this way one can most easily get an idea of its real power.

Notice its power in such a little matter as putting on one's clothes, one's coat, for instance. Almost every one in doing this always puts the same arm first into the sleeve. With some it is the right arm and with some it is the left. Probably very few, if they were asked, could tell which arm they put in first; but as soon as they undertake to do the thing, the arm which commonly goes first makes its movement; and it is only by a strong act of will that it can be made to give way to the other.

Observe, farther, how skill is acquired in any handiwork, so that at last the work goes on better when we are not thinking of it, than when we attend to what we are doing. The fingers of the skillful pianist take care of themselves, and the old ladies can read as they knit.

Notice now the good results of this tendency of habits to become fixed. In some cases, like those to which I have referred, *the life of the person is, in a sense, doubled.* As was just said, the old ladies knit and read or talk at the same time. So in very many things, the body that has been trained does the work while the mind is left free to busy itself as it will.

Another great advantage that springs from the fixity of habits is found

in the fact that, by means of this, *our lives may make real progress.* What we have gained is secured to us.

Think how hard it would be if we had continually to start again from the beginning. How the soldier shrinks when he first goes into a battle; how gladly he would flee. It is said that green soldiers are sometimes placed alternately with those that have been seasoned in many a fight, that the stability of the veterans may keep the raw recruits in their place. The old soldiers have got so in the habit of marching and standing as they are told, that it has become with them a matter of course.

Consider, too, how a man who is in the habit of handling money lets it pass through his hands with hardly a thought of the possibility of keeping any of it. In such cases habit may sometimes be a better safeguard than principle that has not hardened into habit. Principle untrained may sometimes give way to a temptation which habit would withstand.

This fact applies to everything that we do, and to every relation of our lives. We can make a habit of honesty, of industry, of kindliness, of attention, of courtesy, and of whatever we will. Indeed, Aristotle, one of the wisest men of antiquity, defined virtue as a habit of rightdoing.

Consider what power we have thus over our lives. We shape them to a large extent as we choose, and then, through habit, they tend to harden into the shape that we have given them, as the plaster hardens into the shape which the artist has chosen.

The matter has, very obviously, another side. Bad habits form as readily as good ones. I am not sure that they do not form more readily than good ones, because virtues require more effort than faults. We drift into faults; but to make the best life we have to take control of it and guide it.

Indeed, a bad habit is the last thing that most of us are afraid of. We think that we are acting always from our own choice, that it is no matter what we do now, because another time, whenever we wish, we can do differently. But all the while a certain habit is forming and hardening, until at last we find ourselves almost helpless. Thus, even our tastes, our amusements, our selection of books, the tendency even of our most secret thoughts, are becoming fixed, and *we are becoming permanently the persons we meant to be only for the moment.*

If the artist takes such pains with the plaster that he is forming, so that it may harden into a shape of beauty, what care should we take of the habits which are to effect so strongly and permanently our bodies, our minds, and our hearts.

> *"In the civilian world almost nothing has lasting consequences, so you can blunder though life in a kind of daze. You never have to take inventory of the things in your possession and you never have to calculate the ways in which mundane circumstances can play out—can, in fact, kill you. As a result, you lose a sense of the importance of things, the gravity of things. Back home mundane details also have the power to destroy you, but the cause and effect are often spread so far apart that you don't even make the connection; at Restrepo, that connection was impossible to ignore."*
> —Sebastian Junger, from War, *a book detailing the fifteen months the author spent with a platoon of soldiers stationed at Restrepo, a remote outpost in Afghanistan*

Army Field Manual 21-100, 1941

··

When you hear the word *discipline*, chances are the military is one of the first things that comes to mind. And with good reason—learning rigorous self-discipline is one of the central steps in becoming a soldier. At boot camp, recruits are drilled for weeks on everything from making their bed to cleaning their gun. This unforgiving education in discipline is of the utmost importance; when the newly-minted solider heads out into the field, a failure to pay attention to the details can mean the difference between life and death.

The following excerpts from an Army manual published in 1941 are obviously specifically directed at soldiers. But each guideline, when thoughtfully reflected upon, can be applied in some way to civilian life as well.

··

MILITARY DISCIPLINE

27. [Discipline] is the most important thing in the Army. In civil life lack of discipline in a young man may result in his getting into trouble which will cause his parents and teachers regret or sorrow; it may cause a member of an athletic team to be "sent to the bench," or cause an employee to lose his job. In the Army it is far more serious. Here lack of discipline in a soldier may not only cost him his life and the life of his comrades, but cause a military undertaking to fail and his team to be defeated. On the other hand a team of a few well-disciplined soldiers is worth many times a much larger number of undisciplined individuals who are nothing more than an armed mob. History repeatedly shows that without discipline no body of troops can hold its own against a well-directed and well-disciplined enemy.

28. In your work in the Army you may wonder why the officers and noncommissioned officers insist on perfection in what appears to be minor details. Why do rifles have to be carried at just the same angle; why do you have to keep accurately in line; why must your bed be made in a certain way; why must your uniform and equipment be in a prescribed order at all times; why must all officers be saluted with snap and precision? These things are part of your disciplinary training. Their purpose is to teach you obedience, loyalty, team play, personal pride, pride in your organization, respect for the rights of others, love of the flag, and the will to win.

CARE OF CLOTHING

56. Always remember that your uniform is more than a mere suit of clothes that is worn to cover and protect your body. It is the symbol of the honor, the tradition, and the achievements of our Army. The civilian or soldier who is careless in his dress and appearance is probably careless in everything else. You owe it to your comrades, your organization, and your Army to be neat and careful in your appearance, for officers and men of other organizations will judge your company by the impression you make.

57. By being careful of your uniform, you have many advantages over a careless soldier. Your clothing will last longer, you will be neater and better dressed, and you will make a better impression on your comrades and officers.

58. The following information will assist you in the care of your clothing:

    a. Whenever you wear the uniform, either on or off duty, be sure that it is complete and that it conforms to the instructions of your post, camp, or station. Have your shirt, coat, and overcoat buttoned throughout. Keep your uniform clean, neat, and in good repair.

    b. Dandruff, dust, or cigarette ashes on a uniform give a bad impression. If possible, keep a whisk broom in barracks for brushing your uniform. Promptly replace missing buttons and insignia.

    c. Keep your woolen uniforms pressed. This not only improves the appearance of clothing, but actually increases its life.

    d. Clothing not in use should be hung in wall lockers whenever available. If there are no wall lockers, fold your clothing carefully and put it away where it will not accumulate dust. Uniforms that have become wet or damp should not be folded until they are dry. It is also a good idea to inspect clothing before putting it away. Missing

buttons and rips should be attended to as soon as you take off your clothing instead of waiting until it is again needed.

ARMS AND EQUIPMENT

Responsibility For Care

60. The arms and equipment which are issued to you are the property of the United States. They are entrusted to your care for military use during your period of service in the Army. You are responsible for them and it is your duty to see that they are properly cared for in the manner in which your officers and noncommissioned officers will instruct you. At various times you will attend inspections where your company commander, or other officers, will carefully check over your arms and equipment to see that you are taking the proper care of them and that they are clean and in condition for immediate active service. You will find that a little attention each day to the care and cleaning of your arms and equipment will save you time and effort in preparing for these inspections.

61. Your safety and comfort in the field will depend upon the manner in which you keep your arms and equipment. You must take particular care not to lose them, as you may not be able to replace them by the time you will need them most. Before dark, place everything where you can quickly find it in the dark. Remember that carelessness in the protection and condition of your arms and equipment may cost you your life or health, or that of a comrade.

MARCHES

194. One of your principal jobs in the field is marching. Battles take place at indefinite intervals, but marches occur daily. To win battles troops must arrive on the battlefield on time and in good physical condition. To accomplish this they must be able to march.

195. PREPARATIONS.—a. When you learn that your organization is to make a march the next day there are certain things you should attend to

the evening before. See that your canteen is clean and filled with fresh water as there may be little time for this in the morning. Check your personal equipment and see that you have all the articles necessary for personal cleanliness, and for keeping your clothing in repair. This should include towel, soap, toothbrush, pocket comb, small mirror, needles, thread, safety pins, and spare buttons. Check up on the adjustment of your pack straps and belt. A poorly adjusted pack adds to the discomfort and fatigue of a march. You should have at least two pairs of woolen socks without holes or mends. See that your shoes or boots fit comfortably, are in good repair, and well broken in. Never start a march with a new pair of shoes or boots.

Before dark dispose of any trash or debris that may have collected in or around your tent area. This will save you time and effort in the morning, especially if your organization is to break camp before daylight. Our Army takes pride in always leaving a camp site in better condition than we found it.

196. When you fall in to start the march, do it quietly. One of the indications of a well trained organization is the absence of noise and confusion when starting a march. When you are close to the enemy it will be necessary to maintain quiet for your own protection as he will be on the alert for noises which will help him locate your position. Even when you are at a distance from the enemy, or making a practice march in peace, loud talking

CHAPTER SIX

and shouting will disturb civilian communities or troops camped nearby who are trying to rest.

197. CONDUCT OF INDIVIDUALS.— b. You will remember that in chapter 1 it was stated that civilians will judge your organization and the Army by the conduct and appearance of its members in public. This is especially true of troops on the march. Avoid using profane or obscene language or making remarks to civilians. When you do this, you are not only proving that you are lacking in military discipline but are causing your organization to be considered as poorly trained. This is unfair to your comrades.

"In reading the lives of great men, I found that the first victory they won was over themselves ... self-discipline with all of them came first." —Harry S. Truman

My Will Has Been Stronger Than My Flesh
QUOTES FROM HARRY HOUDINI ON DISCIPLINE

Harry Houdini, "The Handcuff King," was a magician and escape artist extraordinaire. He escaped from prison cells, bank safes, straightjackets, coffins, cans and tanks of water, and, of course, any handcuff he was challenged with. His feats were so astounding some believed he was aided by spirits from the great beyond. But the secret to Houdini's success was not mystical, or even magical, it was simply a matter of strict discipline and strenuous practice. He built himself into the man he wanted to be, element by element.

Houdini set out to learn the secrets of every lock in the world, unable to rest until he knew how to pick them all with ease. He took up running, swimming, and biking long distances to build his body and endurance. He took classes on speech and debate to hone his skills as a charismatic showman.

In his home, he built a large
sunken tub in which to practice
escaping underwater and holding
his breath (he got up to over four
minutes). To train himself for stunts
in which he would jump from bridges
into frigid rivers while handcuffed
and shackled, he would add ice to the
water to increase his stamina. When
guests came to visit, he would work a
deck of cards with his fingers or untie
knots with his toes, letting his digits
get a workout while he carried on an
engaging conversation.

Houdini's practice and study ses-
sions were so all-consuming he would
frequently forget to eat and bathe; his wife Bess had to remind him to change
his underwear.

The quotes below clearly show how this rigorous discipline of body and
mind allowed Houdini to attain supreme success.

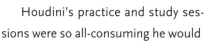

I want to be first. I vehemently want to be first. First in my profession …
For that I give all the thought, all the power, that is in me. To stand at the
head of my rank: it is all I ask … so I have struggled and fought. I have
done and abstained; I have tortured my body and risked my life, only for
that—to have one plank on the stage where they must fall back and cry
"Master!"… I am strong, as you see; strong in flesh, but my will has been
stronger than my flesh. I have struggled with iron and steel, with locks
and chains; I have burned, drowned, and frozen till my body has become
almost insensible to pain; I have done things which rightly I could not do,

because I said to myself, "You must"; and now I am old at 36. A man is only a man, and the flesh revenges itself. Yet the will is its master when the will is strong enough. Do you think that these religious martyrs—the willing martyrs—those in India, say—who torture themselves by driving hooks through their flesh and swinging suspended—do you think they suffer pain? I say "No; they do not." I have proved it in myself. To think vehemently of a thing, of the feat, that conquers the pain—some kinds of pain. If the thought is intense enough, the pain goes—for a time. Sometimes the task before me is very hard. Not every night, but sometimes. I must fling myself down and writhe; I must strive with every piece of force I possess; I bruise and batter myself against the floor, the walls; I strain and sob and exhaust myself, and begin again, and exhaust myself again; but do I feel pain? Never. How can I feel pain? There is no place for it. All my mind is filled with a single thought—to get free! Get free! And the intoxication of that freedom, that success is sublime.

Successive entries from Houdini's journal:

Jan. 7. Gee whiz! Another ice bath. They want to see me earn my money.

Jan. 9. Took cold bath, 49 deg.

Jan. 10. Took cold bath, 48 deg. Doctor stops ice bath.

Jan. 16. Cold bath, 40 deg. Gee, it's cold.

Jan. 18. Taking icy baths to get ready for bridge jump. Water about 36 deg.

My chief task has been to conquer fear. When I am stripped and manacled, nailed securely within a weighted packing case and thrown into the sea, or when I am buried alive under six feet of earth, it is necessary to preserve absolute serenity of spirit … I have to work with great delicacy and lightning speed. If I grow panicky I am lost. And if something goes wrong, if there is some little accident or mishap, some slight miscalculation, I am lost unless all my faculties are working on high, free from mental tension or strain. The public sees only the thrill of the accomplished trick; they have no conception of the tortuous preliminary self-training that was necessary to conquer fear.

My second secret has been, by equally vigorous self-training, to enable me to do remarkable things with my body, to make not one muscle or group of muscles, but *every* muscle a responsive worker, quick and sure for its part, to make my fingers super-fingers in dexterity, and to train my toes to do the work of fingers.

When I was a youngster in petticoats locks had a fascination for me. As I grew up I worked with various locksmiths. The study of locks led to the study of all sorts of locking appliances. In this connection I took up physics, even dipped into chemistry a bit. You know five hours is a full night's sleep for me. I can do with less. It's remarkable what a lot of work a fellow can get done during those three extra hours while the rest of the world is in bed. It's nearly eleven hundred extra hours a year. Maybe that's one of the reasons I am the Great Houdini instead of a side-show piker.

Do But One Thing at Once
A LETTER FROM LORD CHESTERFIELD TO HIS SON, 1747

Lord Chesterfield was a British statesman who penned a series of letters to his son Philip, imparting his advice on topics ranging from political strategy to etiquette. While his son never became the success his father so desperately hoped these letters would help him become, we can benefit from the sage and sometimes witty advice of Lord Chesterfield on how to conduct oneself as a man of the world.

London, April the 14th, O. S. 1747.

DEAR BOY,

You may remember, that I have always earnestly recommended to you, to do what you are about, be that what it will; and to do nothing else at the same time. Do not imagine that I mean by this, that you should attend to, and plod at, your book all day long; far from it: I mean that you should have your pleasures too; and that you should attend to them, for the time, as much as to your studies; and if you do not attend equally to both, you will neither have improvement nor satisfaction from either. A man is fit for neither business nor pleasure who either cannot, or does not, command and direct his attention to the present object, and in some degree banish, for that time, all other objects from his thoughts. If at a ball, a supper, or a party of pleasure, a man were to be solving, in his own mind, a problem in Euclid, he would be a very bad companion, and make a very poor figure in that company; or if, in studying a problem in his closet, he were to think of a minuet, I am apt to believe that he would make a very poor mathematician. There is time enough for everything, in the course of the day, if you do but one thing at once; but there is not time enough in the year, if you will do two things at a time. The Pensionary de Witt, who was torn to pieces in the year 1672, did the whole business of the Republic, and yet had time left to go to assemblies in the evening, and sup in company. Being asked how he could possibly find time to go through so much business, and yet amuse himself in the evenings as he did; he answered, there was nothing so easy; for that it was only doing one thing at a time, and never putting off anything till tomorrow that could be done today. This steady and undissipated attention to one object is a sure mark of a superior genius; as hurry, bustle, and agitation, are the never-failing symptoms of a weak and frivolous mind. When you read Horace, attend to the justness of his thoughts, the happiness of his diction, and the beauty of his poetry; and do not think of Puffendorf *de Homine et Cive:* and when you are reading Puffendorf, do not think of Madame de St. Germain; nor of Puffendorf, when you are talking to Madame de St. Germain.

> *"If unwilling to rise in the morning, say to thyself, 'I awake to do the work of a man.'"* —Marcus Aurelius

You Must Be One Man
FROM *THE ENCHIRIDION*
By Epictetus

Epictetus (55–135 A.D.) was a Greek Stoic philosopher who argued that unhappiness was created by fighting against those events and forces that were not in our power to control. That which *was* within our power to control—our own actions—had to be regulated through discipline and towards virtue in order to attain eudemonia.

In every act observe the things which come first, and those which follow it; and so proceed to the act. If you do not, at first you will approach it with alacrity, without having thought of the things which will follow; but afterwards, when certain base (ugly) things have shown themselves, you will be ashamed. A man wishes to conquer at the Olympic games. I also wish indeed, for it is a fine thing. But observe both the things which come first, and the things which follow; and then begin the act. You must do every thing according to rule, eat according to strict orders, abstain from delicacies, exercise yourself as you are bid at appointed times, in heat, in cold, you must not drink cold water, nor wine as you choose; in a word, you must deliver yourself up to the exercise master as you do to the physician, and then proceed to the contest. And sometimes you will strain the

hand, put the ankle out of
joint, swallow much dust, some-
times be flogged, and after all this be defeated.
When you have considered all this, if you still
choose, go to the contest: if you do not, you
will behave like children, who at one time
play at wrestlers, another time as flute play-
ers, again as gladiators, then as trumpeters,
then as tragic actors: so you also will be at
one time an athlete, at another a gladiator, then
a rhetorician, then a philosopher, but with your
whole soul you will be nothing at all; but like an
ape you imitate every thing that you see, and
one thing after another pleases you. For you
have not undertaken any thing with consideration, nor have you surveyed it well; but carelessly and with cold desire.

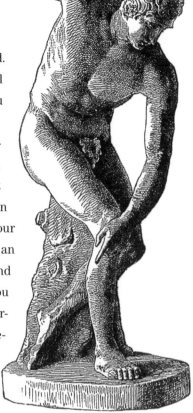

Thus some who have seen a philosopher and having heard one speak, as
Euphrates speaks—and who can speak as
he does?—they wish to be philosophers themselves also. My man, first of
all consider what kind of thing it is: and then examine your own nature,
if you are able to sustain the character. Do you wish to be a pentathlete
or a wrestler? Look at your arms, your thighs, examine your loins. For
different men are formed by nature for different things. Do you think that
if you do these things, you can eat in the same manner, drink in the same
manner, and in the same manner loathe certain things? You must pass
sleepless nights, endure toil, go away from your kinsman, be despised
by a slave, in every thing have the inferior part, in honor, in office in the
courts of justice, in every little matter. Consider these things, if you would
exchange for them, freedom from passions, liberty, tranquility. If not, take

care that, like little children, you be not now a philosopher, then a servant of the publicani, then a rhetorician, then a procurator (manager) for Caesar. These things are not consistent. You must be one man, either good or bad. You must either cultivate your own ruling faculty, or external things; you must either exercise your skill on internal things or on external things; that is you must either maintain the petition of a philosopher or that of a common person.

"The great end of education is to discipline rather than to furnish the mind; to train it to the use of its own powers, rather than fill it with the accumulation of others." —Tyron Edwards

The Pursuit of Mental Efficiency
FROM *MENTAL EFFICIENCY*, 1911
By Arnold Bennett

THE APPEAL

If there is any virtue in advertisements—and a journalist should be the last person to say that there is not—the American nation is rapidly reaching a state of physical efficiency of which the world has probably not seen the like since Sparta. In all the American newspapers and all the American monthlies are innumerable illustrated announcements of "physical-culture specialists," who guarantee to make all the organs of the body perform their duties with the mighty precision of a 60 h.p. motor-car that never breaks down. I saw a book the other day written by one of these specialists, to show how perfect health could be attained by devoting a quarter of an hour a day to certain exercises. The advertisements multiply and increase in size. They cost a great deal of money. Therefore they must bring in a great deal of business. Therefore vast numbers of people must be worried about the non-efficiency of their bodies, and on the way to achieve efficiency. In our more modest British fashion, we have the same phenomenon in

England. And it is growing. Our muscles are growing also. Surprise a man in his bedroom of a morning, and you will find him lying on his back on the floor, or standing on his head, or whirling clubs, in pursuit of physical efficiency. I remember that once I "went in" for physical efficiency myself. I, too, lay on the floor, my delicate epidermis separated from the carpet by only the thinnest of garments, and I contorted myself according to the fifteen diagrams of a large chart (believed to be the *magna charta* of physical efficiency) daily after shaving. In three weeks my collars would not meet round my prize-fighter's neck; my hosier reaped immense profits, and I came to the conclusion that I had carried physical efficiency quite far enough.

A strange thing—was it not?—that I never had the idea of devoting a quarter of an hour a day after shaving to the pursuit of mental efficiency. The average body is a pretty complicated affair, sadly out of order, but happily susceptible to culture. The average mind is vastly more complicated, not less sadly out of order, but perhaps even more susceptible to culture. We compare our arms to the arms of the gentleman illustrated in the physical efficiency advertisement, and we murmur to ourselves the classic phrase: "This will never do." And we set about developing the muscles of our arms until we can show them off (through a frock coat) to women at afternoon tea. But it does not, perhaps, occur to us that the mind has its muscles, and a lot of apparatus besides, and that these invisible, yet paramount, mental organs are far less efficient than they ought to be; that some of them are atrophied, others starved, others out of shape, etc. A man of sedentary occupation goes for a very long walk on Easter Monday, and in the evening is so exhausted that he can scarcely eat. He wakes up to the inefficiency of his body, caused by his neglect of it, and he is so shocked that he determines on remedial measures. Either he will walk to the office, or he will play golf, or he will execute the post-shaving exercises. But let the same man after a prolonged sedentary course of newspapers, magazines, and novels, take his mind out for a stiff climb among the rocks of a scientific, philosophic, or artistic subject. What will he do? Will he stay out all day, and return in the evening too tired even to read his paper? Not he. It is ten to one that, finding himself puffing for breath after a quarter of an hour, he won't even persist till he gets his second wind, but will come back at once. Will he remark with genuine concern that his mind is sadly out of condition and that he really must do something to get it into order? Not he. It is a hundred to one that he will tranquilly accept the *status quo*, without shame and without very poignant regret. Do I make my meaning clear?

I say, without a *very poignant* regret, because a certain vague regret is indubitably caused by realizing that one is handicapped by a mental inefficiency which might, without too much difficulty, be cured. That vague regret exudes like a vapour from the more cultivated section of the public. It is to be detected everywhere, and especially among people who are near the half-way house of life. They perceive the existence of immense quantities of knowledge, not the smallest particle of which will they ever make their own. They stroll forth from their orderly dwellings on a starlit night, and feel dimly the wonder of the heavens. But the still small voice is telling them that, though they have read in a newspaper that there are fifty thousand stars in the Pleiades, they cannot even point to the Pleiades in the sky. How they would like to grasp the significance of the nebular theory, the most overwhelming of all theories! And the years are passing; and there are twenty-four hours in every day, out of which they work only six or seven; and it needs only an impulse, an effort, a system, in order gradually to cure the mind of its slackness, to give "tone" to its muscles, and to enable it to grapple with the splendours of knowledge and sensation that await it! But the regret is not poignant enough. They do nothing. They go on doing nothing. It is as though they passed for ever along the length of an endless table filled with delicacies, and could not stretch out a hand to seize. Do I exaggerate? Is there not deep in the consciousness of most of us a mournful feeling that our minds are like the liver of the advertisement—sluggish, and that for the sluggishness of our minds there is the excuse neither of incompetence, nor of lack of time, nor of lack of opportunity, nor of lack of means?

We have the desire to perfect ourselves, to round off our careers with the graces of knowledge and taste. How many people would not gladly undertake some branch of serious study, so that they might not die under the reproach of having lived and died without ever really having known anything about anything! It is not the absence of desire that prevents them. It is, first, the absence of will-power—not the will to begin, but the will to continue; and, second, a mental apparatus which is out of condition, "puffy," "weedy," through sheer neglect. The remedy, then, divides itself into two parts, the cultivation of will-power, and the getting into condition of the mental apparatus. And these two branches of the cure must be worked concurrently.

THE CURE

Let me take an average case. Let me take your case, O man or woman of thirty, living in comfort, with some cares, and some responsibilities, and some pretty hard daily work, but not too much of any! The question of mental efficiency is in the air. It interests you. It touches you nearly. Your conscience tells you that your mind is less active and less informed than it might be. You suddenly spring up from the garden-seat, and you say to yourself that you will take your mind in hand and do something with it. Wait a moment. Be so good as to sink back into that garden-seat and clutch that tennis racket a little longer. You have had these "hours of insight" before, you know. You have not arrived at the age of thirty without having tried to carry out noble resolutions—and failed. What precautions are you going to take against failure this time? For your will is probably no stronger now than it was aforetime. You have admitted and accepted failure in the past. And no wound is more cruel to the spirit of resolve than that dealt by failure. You fancy the wound closed, but just at the critical moment it may reopen and mortally bleed you. What are your precautions? Have you thought of them? No. You have not.

I have not the pleasure of your acquaintance. But I know you because I know myself. Your failure in the past was due to one or more of three causes. And the first was that you undertook too much at the beginning. You started off with a magnificent programme. You are something of an expert in physical exercises—you would be ashamed not to be, in these physical days—and so you would never attempt a hurdle race or an uninterrupted hour's club-whirling without some preparation. The analogy between the body and the mind ought to have struck you. *This* time, please do not form an elaborate programme. Do not form any programme. Simply content yourself with a preliminary canter, a ridiculously easy preliminary canter. For example (and I give this merely as an example), you might say to yourself: "Within one month from this date I will read twice Herbert Spencer's little book on 'Education'—sixpence—and will make notes in pencil inside the back cover of the things that particularly strike me." You remark that that is nothing, that you can do it "on your head," and so on. Well, do it. When it is done you will at any rate possess the satisfaction of having resolved to do something and having done it. Your mind will have gained tone and healthy pride. You will be even justified in setting yourself some kind of a simple programme to extend over three months. And you will have acquired some general principles by the light of which to construct the programme. But best of all, you will have avoided failure, that dangerous wound.

The second possible cause of previous failure was the disintegrating effect on the will-power of the ironic, superior smile of friends. Whenever a man "turns over a new leaf" he has this inane giggle to face. The drunk-ard may be less ashamed of getting drunk than of breaking to a crony the news that he has signed the pledge. Strange, but true! And human nature must be counted with. Of course, on a few stern spirits the effect of that smile is merely to harden the resolution. But on the majority its influence is deleterious. Therefore don't go and nail your flag to the mast. Don't raise any flag. Say nothing. Work as unobtrusively as you can. When you have won a battle or two you can begin to wave the banner, and then you will find that that miserable, pitiful, ironic, superior smile will die away ere it is born.

The third possible cause was that you did not rearrange your day. Idler and time-waster though you have been, still you had done *something* dur-ing the twenty-four hours. You went to work with a kind of dim idea that there were twenty-six hours in every day. *Something large and definite has to be dropped.* Some space in the rank jungle of the day has to be cleared and swept up for the new operations. Robbing yourself of sleep won't help you, nor trying to "squeeze in" a time for study between two other times. Use the knife, and use it freely. If you mean to read or think half an hour a day, arrange for an hour. A hundred percent margin is not too much for a beginner.

MENTAL CALISTHENICS

I have dealt with the state of mind in which one should begin a serious effort towards mental efficiency, and also with the probable causes of fail-ure in previous efforts. We come now to what I may call the calisthenics of the business, exercises which may be roughly compared to the technical exercises necessary in learning to play a musical instrument. It is curious that a person studying a musical instrument will have no false shame whatever in doing mere exercises for the fingers and wrists while a person who is trying to get his mind into order will almost certainly experience a false shame in going through performances which are undoubtedly good for him. Herein lies one of the great obstacles to mental efficiency. Tell a man that he should join a memory class, and he will hum and haw, and say, as I have already remarked, that memory isn't everything; and, in short, he won't join the memory class, partly from indolence, I grant, but more from false shame. (Is not this true?) He will even hesitate about learning things by heart. Yet there are few mental exercises better than learning great poetry or prose by heart. Twenty lines a week for six months: what a "cure" for debility! The chief, but not the only, merit of learning by heart as an exercise is that it compels the mind to concentrate. And the most important preliminary to self-development is the faculty of concentrating at will. Another excellent exercise is to read a page of no matter-what, and then immediately to write down—in one's own words or in the author's—one's full recollection of it. A quarter of an hour a day! No more! And it works like magic.

This brings me to the department of writing. I am a writer by profession; but I do not think I have any prejudices in favour of the exercise of writing. Indeed, I say to myself every morning that if there is one exercise in the world which I hate, it is the exercise of writing. But I must assert that in my opinion the exercise of writing is an indispensable part of any genuine effort towards mental efficiency. I don't care much what you write, so long as you compose sentences and achieve continuity. There are forty ways of writing in an unprofessional manner, and they are all good. You may keep "a full diary," as Mr. Arthur Christopher Benson says he does. This is one of the least good ways. Diaries, save in experienced hands like those of Mr. Benson, are apt to get themselves done with the very minimum of mental effort. They also tend to an exaggeration of egotism, and if they are left lying about they tend to strife. Further, one never knows when one may not be compelled to produce them in a court of law. A journal is better. Do not ask me to define the difference between a journal and a diary. I will not and I cannot. It is a difference that one feels instinctively. A diary treats exclusively of one's self and one's doings; a journal roams wider, and notes whatever one has observed of interest. A diary relates that one had lobster mayonnaise for dinner and rose the next morning with a headache, doubtless attributable to mental strain. A journal relates that Mrs. _____, whom one took into dinner, had brown eyes, and an agreeable trick of throwing back her head after asking a question, and gives her account of her husband's strange adventures in Colorado, etc. A diary is "All I, I, I, I, itself I," (to quote a line of the transcendental poetry of Mary Baker G. Eddy). A journal is the large spectacle of life. A journal may be special or general. I know a man who keeps a journal of all cases of current superstition which he actually encounters. He began it without the slightest suspicion that he was beginning a document of astounding interest and real scientific value; but such was the fact. In default of a diary or a journal, one may write essays (provided one has the moral courage); or one may simply make notes on the book one reads. Or one may construct anthologies of passages which have made an individual and particular appeal to one's tastes.

After writing comes thinking. (The sequence may be considered odd, but I adhere to it.) In this connexion I cannot do better than quote an admirable letter which I have received from a correspondent who wishes to be known only as "An Oxford Lecturer." The italics (except the last) are mine, not his. He says: "Till a man has got his physical brain completely under his control—*suppressing its too-great receptivity, its tendencies to reproduce idly the thoughts of others, and to be swayed by every passing gust of emotion*—I hold that he cannot do a tenth part of the work that he would then be able to perform with little or no effort. Moreover, work apart, he has not entered upon his kingdom, and unlimited possibilities of future development are barred to him. Mental efficiency can be gained by constant practice in meditation—i.e., by concentrating the mind, say, for but ten minutes daily, but with absolute regularity, on some of the highest thoughts of which it is capable. Failures will be frequent, but they must be regarded with simple indifference and dogged perseverance in the path chosen. If that path be followed *without intermission* even for a few weeks the results will speak for themselves."

So much for the more or less technical processes of stirring the mind from its sloth and making it exactly obedient to the aspirations of the soul. And here I close. Numerous correspondents have asked me to outline a course of reading for them. In other words, they have asked me to particularize for them the aspirations of their souls.

If he can't himself decide on a goal he may as well curl up and expire, for the root of the matter is not in him. I will content myself with pointing out that the entire universe is open for inspection. Too many people fancy that self-development means literature. They associate the higher life with an intimate knowledge of the life of Charlotte Brontë, or the order of the plays of Shakespeare. The higher life may just as well be butterflies, or funeral customs, or county boundaries, or street names, or mosses, or stars, or slugs, as Charlotte Brontë or Shakespeare. Choose what interests you. Lots of finely-organized, mentally-efficient persons can't read Shakespeare at any price, and if you asked them who was the author of *The Tenant of Wildfell Hall* they might proudly answer Emily Brontë, if they didn't say they never heard of it. An accurate knowledge of *any* subject, coupled with a carefully nurtured sense of the relativity of that subject to other subjects, implies an enormous self-development. With this hint I conclude.

CHAPTER SEVEN
HONOR

In its most primitive form, honor is simply the status or reputation of a man in the eyes of others. In the past, honor primarily focused on "saving face," often through the use of violence. If a man tried to diminish your status through insults or physical attacks, you hit back, and hit back hard. Might made right, even if you were in reality the guilty party. In the *Iliad*, Achilles unleashed his wrath on Hector to defend the honor of his fallen friend Patroclus. Up into the late nineteenth century, gentlemen would meet on the "field of honor," dueling to defend any slight (however petty) another man made towards him or the woman he loved.

But over the millennia, the meaning of honor has changed from being primarily about outward appearances to focusing on a man's inner qualities. It isn't enough that others *perceive* a man as being virtuous or truthful, a man must *actually* be good. While vestiges of the primitive form of honor still exist today, honor, for the most part, now means being a man of *integrity*.

The word *integrity* is related to the roots of words like *integrate* and *entire*. In Spanish it is rendered *integro*, meaning "whole." Integrity therefore implies the state of being complete, undivided, intact, and unbroken. We have thus saved this virtue for last because honor pulls and bonds together all the other virtues; it is the mark of a man who has successfully integrated all good principles. His life is a unified whole.

The man of honor is loyal, faithful, and true; he keeps his promises and fulfills his duties. His word is his bond. He does the right thing, even when no one is looking. The man of honor is who he says he is and does what he says he will do. He doesn't deal in rationalizations or excuses and is always willing to own up and take responsibility for his mistakes and failures. He doesn't waver when called upon to make the tough choices. He can go to sleep at night with a clear conscience and look at himself in the mirror without flinching. The man of honor knows who he is and where he is going. In short, the honorable man enjoys the supreme confidence and unsurpassed happiness that comes with having every aspect of one's life knit together in a unity of purpose.

In a world that has lost trust in some of its most sacred and important institutions, honor is the virtue most needed and yet in shortest supply. More than ever, we need men of honor who will step up and stand for truth and right. We hope this final chapter solidifies your desire to integrate the manly virtues more fully into your life and to become a part of the growing movement of men seeking to revive the lost art of manliness.

"A man's got to have a code, a creed to live by, no matter his job." —John Wayne

Three Codes of Honor

Communities often establish formal codes of honor that furnish members with a set of standards by which to live while also fostering a sense of solidarity. Below we provide examples of the honor codes of three different groups.

THE WEST POINT CADET CODE
The Cadet Code defines the "minimum standard of ethical behavior that all cadets have contracted to live by." Cadets are expected to strive to live the Spirit

of the Code, which goes beyond this standard to encompass a life of full honor and integrity. The three rules of thumb are designed to help cadets decide whether an action is honorable or not.

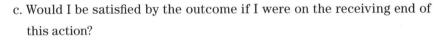

The Cadet Code

"A cadet will not lie, cheat, steal, or tolerate those who do."

Three Rules of Thumb

a. Does this action attempt to deceive anyone or allow anyone to be deceived?

b. Does this action gain or allow the gain of privilege or advantage to which I or someone else would not otherwise be entitled?

c. Would I be satisfied by the outcome if I were on the receiving end of this action?

THE BOY SCOUT OATH AND LAW

The Boy Scouts of America have been pledging the same oath and striving to live the same law for one hundred years.

The Oath

On my honor, I will do my best
To do my duty to God and my country and to obey the Scout Law;
To help other people at all times;
To keep myself physically strong, mentally awake and morally straight.

The Law

A Scout is trustworthy, loyal, helpful, friendly, courteous, kind, obedient, cheerful, thrifty, brave, clean, and reverent.

....

OATH OF THE KNIGHTS OF THE ROUND TABLE

The oath taken by King Arthur and his band of noble knights, as imagined by Howard Pyle in his retelling of their legendary tales.

....

Then all the knights arose, and each knight held up before him the cross of the hilt of his sword, and each knight spake word for word as King Arthur spake. And this was the covenant of their Knighthood of the Round Table: That they would be gentle unto the weak; that they would be courageous unto the strong; that they would be terrible unto the wicked and the evil-doer; that they would defend the helpless who should call upon them for aid; that all women should be held unto them sacred; that they would stand unto the defence of one another whensoever such defence should be required; that they would be merciful unto all men; that they would be gentle of deed, true in friendship, and faithful in love. This was their covenant, and unto it each knight sware upon the cross of his sword, and in witness thereof did kiss the hilt thereof.

> *"A man's character is the reality of himself; his reputation, the opinion others have formed about him; character resides in him, reputation in other people; that is the substance, this is the shadow."* —Henry Ward Beecher

Character Is the Measure of the Man

FROM *THE SUCCESSFUL MAN IN HIS MANIFOLD RELATIONS WITH LIFE*, 1886
By J. Clinton Ransom

Passing along the paths of a cemetery and reading the inscriptions upon the tombstones, one is impressed with the fact that men are soon forgotten when they die. They are laid to rest and their names chronicled upon slabs and statues to mark the place where they lie. But the statues do not preserve their names any more than they do the lifeless limbs slowly crumbling to dust beneath. Only one, or perhaps two, in a thousand dead will live in the memory of those who come after. Only these are deemed worthy to have their names written upon the page of history. The other countless dead are all forgotten almost as soon as the grass grows green upon their graves. The few live on in worthy deeds, the many die because there is nothing to live for. This persistence of worthy living in the memory of men is a good illustration of the eternal persistence of character. In life, people never fully understand the workings of this law.

But character is only the final result of life. It is the end attained after life's activities are over. It is the culmination of principle carried into deeds. It has been forming since we drew our first breath, and shall be forming until the dews of death have fallen upon the eyelids. And at last the character is the measure of the man. All that a man is and does; his habits and appetites; his imaginings, reasonings and memories; his faith, his hope, his love, are blended together in character, as wires are sometimes united under a trip-hammer into a bar of steel.

Character is, then, a blending of many elements, a composite growth of principle, action and sentiment, and when complete it represents that which is permanent in the life of a man. Then character comes to have a reflex action upon life; its effect is cumulative and tends to become settled in certain fixed lines of principle and duty. It is this that makes character the final test of manhood, and gives it a value in successful life; for when these lines of duty are once definitely marked out the man does not easily depart from them, and men come to have confidence in his integrity and ability. When a man has shown that he acts right under a given emergency, such is our confidence in this permanence of character, that we instinctively believe that he will continue to act rightly to the end of life. Good character then is a priceless possession and the best possible exponent of a good and honorable career. It is, indeed, according to the stability and might of this character that one succeeds or fails. No matter how ingenuous the toil of labor, or how transcendent the accomplishment to

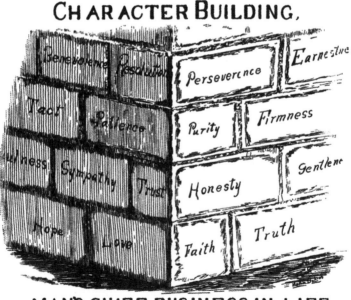

CHARACTER BUILDING,

MAN'S CHIEF BUSINESS IN LIFE.

one of trivial character, if there be no force behind them, both are thrown away and wasted. Character is the force behind the keen-edged tools that accomplishes the work. If it be founded upon principles of eternal truth, it is well.

"Do not consider anything for your interest which makes you break your word, quit your modesty, or inclines you to any practice which will not bear the light, or look the world in the face." —Marcus Aurelius

Myself

FROM *THE FRIENDLY WAY*, 1917
By Edgar Guest

I have to live with myself, and so
I want to be fit for myself to know;
I want to be able as days go by
Always to look myself straight in the eye;
I don't want to stand with the setting sun
And hate myself for the things I've done.

I don't want to keep on a closet shelf
A lot of secrets about myself,
And fool myself as I come and go
Into thinking that nobody else will know
The kind of man I really am;
I don't want to dress myself up in sham.

I want to go out with my head erect,
I want to deserve all men's respect;
But here in the struggle for fame and pelf,
I want to be able to like myself.

I don't want to think as I come and go
That I'm bluster and bluff and empty show.

I never can hide myself from me,
I see what others may never see,
I know what others may never know,
I never can fool myself—and so,
Whatever happens, I want to be
Self-respecting and conscience free.

Do Your Duty in All Things
A LETTER FROM ROBERT E. LEE TO HIS SON, 1852

• •

George Washington Custis Lee was nineteen years old and attending West Point when he received this letter from his father.

• •

Arlington House, April 5, 1852

My dear Son:

I am just in the act of leaving for New Mexico. My fine old regiment has been ordered to that distant region, and I must hasten to see that they are properly taken care of. I have but little to add in reply to your letter of March 26. Your letters breathe a true spirit of frankness; they have given myself and your mother great pleasure.

You must study to be frank with the world, frankness is the child of honest courage. Say what you mean to do on every occasion, and take it for granted you mean to do right. If a friend should ask a favor, you should grant it, if it is possible and reasonable, if not, tell him plainly why you cannot. You will wrong him and yourself by equivocation of any kind. Never do a wrong thing to make a friend or keep one. The man who requires you to do so is dearly purchased at a sacrifice. Deal kindly but firmly with all your classmates. You will find it the policy which wears best. Above all do not appear to others what you are not. If you have any fault to find with anyone, tell him, not others, of what you complain. There is no more dangerous experiment than that of undertaking to be one thing before a man's face and another behind his back. We should live and act and say nothing to injure of any one. It is not only best as a matter of principle but it is the path to peace and honor.

In regard to duty, let me in conclusion of this hasty letter, inform you that nearly a hundred years ago there was a day of remarkable gloom and darkness, still known as the dark day, a day when the light of the sun was slowly extinguished as if by an eclipse. The legislature of Connecticut was in session and as its members saw the unexpected and unaccountable darkness coming on, they shared in the general awe and terror. It was supposed by many that the day of judgment had come. Some one in the consternation of the hour moved for an adjournment. Then there arose an old patriotic legislator, Davenport of Stamford, who said that if the last day had come, he desired to be found in his place of duty, and therefore moved that candles be brought in so that the house could proceed with its duty. There was quietness in that man's mind, the quietness of heavenly wisdom, an inflexible willingness to obey his duty. Duty, then is the sublimest word in our language. Do your duty in all things, like the old puritan. You cannot do more, you should never wish to do less. Let not me or your mother wear one gray hair for any lack of duty on your part.

Your affectionate father,
R.E. LEE.

Self-Measuring Questions Concerning the Characteristic of Integrity

FROM *HOW TO CHOOSE THE RIGHT VOCATION*, 1917
By Holmes W. Merton

Am I conscientious or careless in meeting my financial obligations? When pressed for sufficient money for current expenses, do I spend what money I may get on my own enjoyment or do I apply it in settlement of my accounts with the butcher, grocer and tailor?

Am I punctual, dependable, and strictly honest or am I dilatory, unreliable and unregardful of other people's time, energies and belongings?

Do I believe in scrupulously "sticking to the truth?" Do I report conversations, incidents and things that I have read with fine respect for the truth— and, if I can not remember the facts distinctly, do I frankly admit it; or do I "embroider the facts as pleases my fancy or to win favor with my hearers?"

In my mind does "putting the best foot forward" mean taking one's misfortunes as graciously as may be and making the most of limited means and opportunity or does it imply stretching the truth in self-justification or pushing one's interest to the detriment of others?

Having made an agreement or appointment and, later, desiring to break it, do I do so in a straightforward manner or do I invent seemingly plausible excuses for breaking it?

Does an injury or injustice inflicted upon another arouse my indignation or do I mentally say, "It's no concern of mine?"

When I have made a mistake or have misinterpreted the acts or motives of another, am I willing to acknowledge my error and *desirous* to make reparation if it be possible to do so?

Am I as faithful when working for an employer as when working solely for my own profit?

Can I fearlessly scrutinize my ulterior motives and my business dealings or do I sometimes salve my conscience with the sophistry "business is business?"

If I were an employer and had the power, would I feel justified in grinding my employees down to the lowest living wage?

Am I spontaneously frank and direct in my social and business relations or am I evasive, suave or hypocritical?

Do I possess an integral conscience or have I one section for Sundays and religion and another section for week-days and business?

"A faithful friend is the true image of the Deity."
—Napoleon Bonaparte

The Goatherd and the Wild Goats
An Aesop's Fable

A goatherd, driving his flock from their pasture at eventide, found some wild goats mingled among them, and shut them up together with his own for the night. On the morrow it snowed very hard, so that he could not take the herd to their usual feeding places, but was obliged to keep them in the fold. He gave his own goats just sufficient food to keep them alive, but fed the strangers more abundantly, in the hope of enticing them to stay with him, and of making them his own. When the thaw set in, he led them all out to feed, and the wild goats scampered away as fast as they could to the mountains. The Goatherd taxed them with their ingratitude in leaving him, when during the storm he had taken more care of them than of his own herd. One of them turning about said to him: "That is the very reason why we are so cautious; for if you yesterday treated us better than the Goats you have had so long, it is plain also that if others came after us, you would in the same manner, prefer them to ourselves."

Old friends cannot with impunity be sacrificed for new ones.

"I have been asked what I mean by 'word of honor.' I will tell you. Place me behind prison walls—walls of stone ever so high, ever so thick, reaching ever so far into the ground— there is a possibility that in some way or another I might be able to escape; but stand me on the floor and draw a chalk line around me and have me give my word of honor never to cross it. Can I get out of that circle? No, never! I'd die first."
—Karl G. Maeser

A Letter from George Washington to His Wife, 1775

Shortly before her death, Martha Washington destroyed nearly every letter written between she and her husband. Two of the few remaining letters, including the one below, were found caught behind the drawer of a desk inherited by

Martha's granddaughter. In this letter, written upon being made Commander-in-Chief of the Army, Washington demonstrates his desire to honorably fulfill his two dominating duties—one to his wife, one to his country.

The letter's original spelling and punctuation has been retained.

• •

Philadelphia June 18th 1775

My Dearest,

I am now set down to write to you on a subject which fills me with inexpressable concern—and this concern is greatly aggravated and Increased when I reflect on the uneasiness I know it will give you—It has been determined in Congress, that the whole army raised for the defence of the American Cause shall be put under my care, and that it is necessary for me to proceed immediately to Boston to take upon me the Command of it. —You may beleive me my dear Patcy, when I assure you, in the most solemn manner, that, so far from seeking this appointment I have used every endeavour in my power to avoid it, not only from my unwillingness to part with you and the Family, but from a consciousness of its being a trust too great for my Capacity, and that I should enjoy more real happiness and felicity in one month with you, at home, than I have the most distant prospect of reaping abroad, if my stay was to be Seven times Seven years. —But, as it has been a kind of destiny that has thrown me upon this Service, I shall hope that my undertaking of it, is designd to answer some good purpose—You might, & I suppose did perceive, from the Tenor of my Letters, that I was apprehensive I could not avoid this appointment, as I did not even pretend [to] intimate when I should return—that was the case—it was utterly out of my power to refuse this appointment without exposing my Character to such censures as would have reflected dishonour upon myself, and given pain to my friends—This I am sure could not, & ought not to be pleasing to you, & must have lessend me considerably in my own esteem. —I shall rely therefore, confidently, on that Providence which has heretofore preservd, & been bountiful to me, not doubting but that I shall return safe to you in the fall—I shall feel no pain from the Toil, or the danger of the Campaign—My unhappiness will flow, from the uneasiness I know you will feel at being left alone—I therefore beg of you to summon your whole fortitude & Resolution, and pass your time as agreeably as possible—nothing will give me so much sincere satisfaction as to hear this, and to hear it from your own Pen

If it should be your desire to remove into Alexandria (as you once mentioned upon an occasion of this sort) I am quite pleased that you should put it in practice, & Lund Washington may be directed, by you, to build a Kitchen and other Houses there proper for your Reception—if on the other hand you should rather Incline to spend good part of your time among your Friends below, I wish you to do so—In short, my earnest, & ardent desire is, that you would pursue any Plan that is most likely to produce content, and a tolerable degree of Tranquility as it must add greatly to my uneasy feeling to hear that you are dissatisfied, & complaining at what I really could not avoid.

As Life is always uncertain, and common prudence dictates to every Man the Necessity of settling his temporal Concerns whil[st] it is in his power—and whilst the Mind is calm and undisturbed, I have, since I came to this place (for I had not time to do it before I left home) got Col. Pendleton to Draft a Will for me by the directions which I gave him, which Will I now Inclose—The Provision made for you, in ca[se] of my death, will, I hope, be agreeable.

I shall add nothing more at present as I have several Letters to write, but to desire you will remember me to Milly & all Friends, and to assure you that I am with most unfeigned regard, My dear Patcy

Yr Affecte.

G. Washington

The Builders

FROM *THE SEASIDE AND THE FIRESIDE*, 1850
By Henry Wadsworth Longfellow

All are architects of Fate,
Working in these walls of Time;
Some with massive deeds and great,
Some with ornaments of rhyme.

Nothing useless is, or low;
Each thing in its place is best;
And what seems but idle show
Strengthens and supports the rest.

For the structure that we raise,
Time is with materials filled;
Our to-days and yesterdays
Are the blocks with which we build.

Truly shape and fashion these;
Leave no yawning gaps between;
Think not, because no man sees,
Such things will remain unseen.

In the elder days of Art,
Builders wrought with greatest care
Each minute and unseen part;
For the Gods see everywhere.

Let us do our work as well,
Both the unseen and the seen;
Make the house, where Gods may dwell,
Beautiful, entire, and clean.

Else our lives are incomplete,
Standing in these walls of Time,
Broken stairways, where the feet
Stumble as they seek to climb.

Build to-day, then, strong and sure,
With a firm and ample base;
And ascending and secure
Shall to-morrow find its place.

Thus alone can we attain
To those turrets, where the eye
Sees the world as one vast plain,
And one boundless reach of sky.

"It is part of a good man to do great and noble deeds, though he risk everything." —Plutarch

How a Slave Was Made a Man
FROM *NARRATIVE OF THE LIFE OF FREDERICK DOUGLASS, AN AMERICAN SLAVE*, 1845
By Frederick Douglass

• •

Frederick Douglass was born a slave in 1818. When he was sixteen, his master, unhappy with Douglass, sent him to Edward Covey, who had a reputation for breaking rebellious slaves with brutal punishment. Covey whipped Douglass nearly every week and worked him to the bone, leaving Douglass feeling broken "body, soul, and spirit" and close to suicide. But then one day Douglass reached his limit, stood up for his honor, and reclaimed his manhood.

••

I have already intimated that my condition was much worse during the first six months of my stay at Mr. Covey's than in the last six. The circumstances leading to the change in Mr. Covey's course toward me form an epoch in my humble history. You have seen how a man was made a slave; you shall see how a slave was made a man.

Mr. Covey was at the house, about one hundred yards from the treading-yard where we were fanning. On hearing the fan stop, he left immediately, and came to the spot where we were. He hastily enquired what the matter was. Bill answered that I was sick, and there was no one to bring wheat to the fan. I had by this time crawled away under the side of the post and rail-fence by which the yard was enclosed, hoping to find relief by getting out of the sun. He then asked where I was. He was told by one of the hands. He came to the spot, and after looking at me awhile, asked me what was the matter. I told him as well as I could, for I scarce had strength to speak. He then gave me a savage kick in the side, and told me to get up. I tried to do so, but fell back in the attempt. He gave me another kick, and again told me to rise. I again tried, and succeeded in gaining my feet: but, stooping to get the tub with which I was feeding the fan, I again staggered and fell. While down in this situation, Mr. Covey took up the hickory slat with which Hughes had been striking off the half-bushel measure, and with it gave me a heavy blow upon the head, making a large wound, and the blood ran freely; and with this, again told me to get up. I made no effort to comply, having now made up my mind to let him do his worst.

In a short time after receiving this blow, my head grew better. Mr. Covey had now left me to my fate. At this moment I resolved, for the first time, to go to my master, enter a complaint, and ask his protection. In order to do this, I must that afternoon walk seven miles; and this, under the circumstances, was truly a severe undertaking. I was exceedingly feeble; made so as much by the kicks and blows which I received, as by the severe fit of sickness to which I had been subjected. I, however, watched my chance, while Covey was looking in an opposite direction, and started for St. Michael's. I succeeded in getting a considerable distance on my way to the woods, when Covey discovered me, and called after me to come back, threatening what he would do if I did not come. I disregarded both his calls and his threats, and made my way to the woods as fast as my feeble state would allow; and thinking I might be overhauled by him if I kept the road, I walked through the woods, keeping far enough from the road to avoid detection, and near enough to prevent losing my way. I had not gone far, before my little strength again failed me. I could go no farther. I fell down, and lay for a considerable time. The blood was yet oozing from the wound on my head. For a time I thought I should bleed to death, and think now that I should have done so, but that the blood so matted my hair as to stop the wound.

After lying there about three quarters of an hour, I nerved myself up again, and started on my way, through bogs and briers, barefooted and bareheaded, tearing my feet sometimes at nearly every step; and after a journey of about seven miles, occupying some five hours to perform it, I arrived at master's store. I then presented an appearance enough to affect any but a heart of iron. From the crown of my head to my feet, I was covered with blood. My hair was all clotted with dust and blood; my shirt was stiff with blood. My legs and feet were torn in sundry places with briers and thorns, and were also covered with blood. I suppose I looked like a man who had escaped a den of wild beasts, and barely escaped them. In this state I appeared before my master, humbly entreating him to interpose his authority for my protection. I told him all the circumstances as well as I could, and it seemed, as I spoke, at times to affect him. He would then walk the floor, and seek to justify Covey by saying he expected I deserved it. He asked me what I wanted. I told him to let me get a new home; that as sure as I lived with Mr. Covey again, I should live with but to die with him; that Covey would surely kill me—he was in a fair way for it. Master Thomas ridiculed the idea that there was any danger of Mr. Covey's killing me, and said that he knew Mr. Covey; that he was a good man, and that he could not think of taking me from him; that should he do so, he would lose the whole year's wages; that I belonged to Mr. Covey for one year, and that I must go back to him, come what might; and that I must not trouble him with any more stories, or that he would himself *get hold of me*. After threatening me thus, he gave me a very large dose of salts, telling me that I might remain in St. Michael's that night, (it being quite late,) but that I must be off back to Mr. Covey's early in the morning; and that if I did not, he would *get hold of me*, which meant that he would whip me. I remained all night, and according to his orders, I started off to Covey's in the morning ... wearied in body and broken in spirit.

Upon entering the yard gate, out came Mr. Covey on his way to meeting. He spoke to me very kindly, bade me drive the pigs from a lot near by, and passed on towards the church. ... All went well till Monday morning. ... Long before daylight, I was called to go and rub, curry, and feed the horses. I obeyed, and was glad to obey. But whilst thus engaged, whilst in the act of throwing down some blades from the loft, Mr. Covey entered the stable with a long rope; and just as I was half out of the loft, he caught hold of my legs, and was about tying me. As soon as I found what he was up to, I gave a sudden spring, and as I did so, he holding to my legs, I was brought sprawling on the stable floor. Mr. Covey seemed now to think he had me, and could do what he pleased; but at this moment—from whence came the spirit I don't know—I resolved to fight; and suiting my action to the resolution, I seized Covey hard by the throat; and as I did so, I rose. He held on to me, and I to him. My resistance was so entirely unexpected, that Covey seemed taken all aback. He trembled like a leaf. This gave me assurance, and I held him uneasy, causing the blood to run where I touched him with the ends of my fingers. Mr. Covey soon called out to Hughes for help. Hughes came, and, while Covey held me, attempted to tie my right hand. While he was in the act of doing so, I watched my chance, and gave him a heavy kick close under the ribs. This kick fairly sickened Hughes, so that he left me in the hands of Mr. Covey. This kick had the effect of not only weakening Hughes, but Covey also. When he saw Hughes bending over with pain, his courage quailed. He asked me if I meant to persist in my resistance. I told him I did, come what might; that he had used me like a brute for six months, and that I was determined to be used so no longer. With that, he strove to drag me to a stick that was lying just out of the stable door. He meant to knock me down. But just as he was leaning over to get the stick, I seized him with both hands by his collar, and brought him by a sudden snatch to the ground. By this time, Bill came. Covey called upon him for assistance. Bill wanted to know what he could do. Covey said, "Take hold of him, take hold of him!" Bill said his master hired him out to work, and not to help to whip me; so he left Covey and myself to fight our own battle out. We were at it for nearly two hours. Covey at length let me go, puffing and blowing at a great rate, saying that if I had not resisted, he would not have whipped me half so much. The truth was, that he had not whipped me at all. I considered him as getting entirely the worst end of the bargain; for he had drawn no blood from me, but I had from him. The whole six months afterwards, that I spent with Mr. Covey, he never laid the weight of his finger upon me in anger. He would occasionally say, he didn't want to get hold of me again. "No," thought I, "you need not; for you will come off worse than you did before."

This battle with Mr. Covey was the turning-point in my career as a slave. It rekindled the few expiring embers of freedom, and revived within me a sense of my own manhood. It recalled the departed self-confidence, and inspired me again with a determination to be free. The gratification afforded by the triumph was a full compensation for whatever else might follow, even death itself. He only can understand the deep satisfaction which I experienced, who has himself repelled by force the bloody arm of slavery. I felt as I never felt before. It was a glorious resurrection from the tomb of slavery to the heaven of freedom. My long-crushed spirit rose, cowardice departed, bold defiance took its place; and I now resolved that, however long I might remain a slave in form, the day had passed for ever when I could be a slave in fact. I did not hesitate to let it be known of me, that the white man who expected to succeed in whipping, must also succeed in killing me.

"I hope I shall always possess firmness and virtue enough to maintain what I consider the most enviable of all titles, the character of an honest man."
—George Washington

Be in Earnest
FROM THE INAUGURAL ADDRESS OF THE LORD RECTOR
OF THE UNIVERSITY OF GLASGOW
By Lord Bulwer Lytton, 1856

Never affect to be other than you are—either richer or wiser. Never be ashamed to say, "I do not know." Men will then believe you when you say, "I do know."

Never be ashamed to say, whether as applied to time or money, "I cannot afford it"—"I cannot afford to waste an hour in the idleness to which you invite me—I cannot afford the guinea you ask me to throw away."

Learn to say "No" with decision, "Yes" with caution; "No" with decision whenever it resists a temptation; "Yes" with caution whenever it implies a promise. A promise once given is a bond inviolable.

A man is already of consequence in the world when it is known that we can implicitly rely upon him. I have frequently seen in life a person preferred to a long list of applicants for some important charge, which lifts him at once into station and fortune, merely because he has this reputation—that when he says he knows a thing, he knows it, and when he says he will do a thing, he will do it.

"In great matters men show themselves as they wish to be seen; in small matters, as they are." —Nicolas Chamfort

The Brand of Honesty
FROM THE SPEECH, *CITIZENSHIP IN A REPUBLIC*, 1910
By Theodore Roosevelt

The very last thing that an intelligent and self-respecting member of a democratic community should do is to reward any public man because that public man says he will get the private citizen something to which this private citizen is not entitled, or will gratify some emotion or animosity which this private citizen ought not to possess. Let me illustrate this by one anecdote from my own experience.

A number of years ago I was engaged in cattle-ranching on the great plains of the western United States. There were no fences. The cattle wandered free, the ownership of each being determined by the brand; the calves were branded with the brand of the cows they followed. If on the round-up an animal was passed by, the following year it would appear as an unbranded yearling, and was then called a maverick. By the custom of the country these mavericks were branded with the brand of the man on whose range they were found.

One day I was riding the range with a newly hired cowboy, and we came upon a maverick. We roped and threw it; then we built a little fire, took out a cinch-ring, heated it at the fire; and the cowboy started to put on the brand. I said to him, "It is So-and-so's brand," naming the man on whose range we happened to be. He answered, "That's all right, boss; I know my business." In another moment I said to him, "Hold on, you are putting on my brand!" To which he answered, "That's all right: I always put on the boss's brand." I answered, "Oh, very well. Now you go straight back to the ranch and get what is owing to you; I don't need you any longer." He jumped up and said, "Why, what's the matter? I was putting on your brand." And I answered, "Yes, my friend, and if you will steal *for* me you will steal *from* me."

Now, the same principle which applies in private life applies also in public life. If a public man tries to get your vote by saying that he will do something wrong *in* your interest, you can be absolutely certain that if ever it becomes worth his while he will do something wrong *against* your interest.

> *"When a man takes an oath, Meg, he's holding his own self in his own hands. Like water. And if he opens his fingers then— he needn't hope to find himself again."* —Sir Thomas More *(from* A Man for All Seasons *by playwright Robert Bolt)*

My Honor Is My Own
THE SPEECH OF MARCUS ATILIUS REGULUS TO THE ROMAN SENATE
By Epes Sargent

· ·

In 255 B.C., during the war with Carthage, the Roman general Regulus was taken prisoner. After five years, he was released to return to Rome in order to ask the Senate for peace or an exchange of prisoners. If this plea were accepted, Regulus would be liberated. If it were not, he gave his word he would return to Carthage. On appearing before the Roman Senate, to the astonishment of his Carthaginian captors, he advised Rome *against* their enemy's overtures of peace. Despite the pleadings of his friends and family, he chose to return to captivity, where he suffered cruel torture and death rather than break his oath.

· ·

Ill does it become *me*, O Senators of Rome!— ill does it become Regulus— after having so often stood in this venerable Assembly clothed with the supreme dignity of the Republic, to stand before you a captive—the captive of Carthage! Though outwardly I am free—though no fetters encumber the limbs, or gall the flesh—yet the heaviest of chains—the pledge of a Roman Consul—makes me the bondsman of the Carthaginians. They have my promise to return to them, in the event of the failure of this their embassy. My life is at their mercy. My honor is my own—a possession which no reverse of fortune can jeopard; a flame which imprisonment cannot stifle, time cannot dim, death cannot extinguish.

Of the train of disasters which followed close on the unexampled successes of our arms—of the bitter fate which swept off the flower of our soldiery, and consigned me, your General, wounded and senseless, to Carthaginian keeping—I will not speak. For five years, a rigorous captivity has been my portion. For five years, the society of family and friends, the dear amenities of home, the sense of freedom, and the sight of country, have been to me a recollection and a dream—no more! But during that period Rome has retrieved her defeats. She has recovered under Metellus what under Regulus she lost. She has routed armies. She has taken unnumbered prisoners. She has struck terror to the hearts of the Carthaginians; who have now sent me hither with their Ambassadors, to sue for peace, and to propose that, in exchange for me, your former Consul, a thousand common prisoners of war shall be given up. You have heard the Ambassadors. Their intimations of some unimaginable horror—I know not what—impending over myself, should I fail to induce you to accept their terms, have strongly moved your sympathies in my behalf. Another appeal, which I would you might have been spared, has lent force to their suit. A wife and children, threatened with widowhood and orphanage, weeping and despairing, have knelt at your feet, on the very threshold of the Senate-chamber. Conscript Fathers! Shall not Regulus be saved? Must he return to Carthage to meet the cruelties which the Ambassadors brandish before our eyes? With one voice you answer, No! Countrymen! Friends! For all that I have suffered—for all that I may have to suffer—I am repaid in the compensation of this moment! Unfortunate, you may hold me; but, O, not undeserving! Your confidence in my honor survives all the ruin that adverse fortune could inflict. You have not forgotten the past. Republics are not ungrateful! May the thanks I cannot utter bring down blessings from the Gods on you and Rome!

Conscript Fathers! There is but one course to be pursued. Abandon all thought of peace. Reject the overtures of Carthage! Reject them wholly and unconditionally! What! Give back to her a thousand able-bodied men, and receive in return this one attenuated, war-worn, fever-wasted frame—this weed, whitened in a dungeon's darkness, pale and sapless, which no kindness of the sun, no softness of the summer breeze, can ever restore to health and vigor?

It must not—it shall not be! O! were Regulus what he was once, before captivity had unstrung his sinews and enervated his limbs, he might pause—he might proudly think he were well worth a thousand of the foe—he might say, "Make the exchange! Rome shall not lose by it!" But now—alas! Now 'tis gone—that impetuosity of strength, which could once make him a leader indeed, to penetrate a phalanx or guide a pursuit.

His very armor would be a burden now. His battle-cry would be drowned in the din of the onset. His sword would fall harmless on his opponent's shield. But, if he cannot *live*, he can at least *die*, for his country! Do not deny him this supreme consolation. Consider: every indignity, every torture, which Carthage shall heap on his dying hours, will be better than a trumpet's call to your armies. They will remember only Regulus, their fellow-soldier and their leader. They will forget his defeats. They will regard only his services to the Republic. Tunis, Sardinia, Sicily—every well-fought field, won by *his* blood and *theirs*—will flash on their remembrance, and kindle their avenging wrath. And so shall Regulus, though dead, fight as he never fought before against the foe.

Conscript Fathers! There is another theme. My family—forgive the thought! To you, and to Rome, I confide them. I leave them no legacy but my name—no testament but my example.

Ambassadors of Carthage! I have spoken, though not as you expected. I am your captive. Lead me back to whatever fate may await me. Doubt not that you shall find, to Roman hearts, country is dearer than life, and integrity more precious than freedom!

"It is better to deserve honors and not have them than to have them and not deserve them." —Mark Twain

CHAPTER SEVEN

The Better Thing

By Anonymous

It is better to lose with a conscience clean

Than to win by a trick unfair;

It is better to fail and to know you've been,

Whatever the prize was, square,

Than to claim the joy of a far-off goal

And the cheers of the standers-by,

And to know down deep in your inmost soul

A cheat you must live and die.

Who wins by trick can take the prize,

And at first he may think it sweet,

But many a day in the future lies

When he'll wish he had met defeat.

For the man who lost shall be glad at heart

And walk with his head up high.

While his conqueror knows he must play the part

Of a cheat and a living lie.

The prize seems fair when the fight is on,

But unless it is truly won

You will hate the thing when the crowds are gone,

HONOR

For it stands for a false deed done.

And it's better you never should reach your goal

Than ever success to buy

At the price of knowing down in your soul

That your glory is all a lie.

Words and Deeds

FROM *BEOWULF*, IN *GUDRUN, BEOWULF AND ROLAND*
WITH OTHER MEDIEVAL TALES, 1884
By John Gibb

• •

In this selection from a re-telling of the over 1,000-year-old epic poem, the courageous warrior Beowulf comes to the aid of King Hrothgar, who is tormented by
a monster named Grendel who comes to the royal hall of Heorot and devours
the king's men. On the night Beowulf is slated to take on Grendel, he defends
himself from the heckling of Hunferth, who thinks Beowulf isn't strong enough
to defeat the seemingly unstoppable beast. In his reply, Beowulf demonstrates
the dishonor of the man who criticizes others without having done anything
himself, sets the record straight about his heroic feats, and promises to kill
Grendel, a boast he will shortly make good on, showing that the man of honor
backs up his words with real deeds.

• •

The heroes entered the hall of Heorot, where upon a lofty seat sat Hrothgar
ready to receive them. Beowulf spake and said—

"Hail to thee, Hrothgar, King of the Danes! I am the kinsman and the thane
of Hygelac, King of the Geatas. The deeds of Grendel became known to me
when I was dwelling at home, and wise men counselled me to go to your
help. I am strong, and have done many mighty deeds. It was I that destroyed
the Jotuns, and who slew the Nicors by night. Alone will I meet this wretch
Grendel. I ask this one favour of thee, O King, that thou wilt commit to me
and to my companions the task of cleansing Heorot from the foul foe."

Hrothgar answered and said, "Thou hast come as a defence to my land, Beowulf. I am filled with sorrow and shame. Grendel has robbed me of my warriors, and no one dare any more tarry in Heorot after the light of the sun departs. Thou art welcome, since thou hast come to meet the destroyer. Sit down on the benches of the hall, and join in our feasting before thou goest to encounter the enemy."

A bench was cleared in the hall for Beowulf and for his companions, and they sat down and drank the bright ale which was poured out for them from the flagon. A bard raised his voice and sang with a clear voice, and all the warriors rejoiced together, and there was great gladness throughout the hall.

But Hunferth, the son of Ecglaf, who sat at the feet of King Hrothgar, was displeased. He was grieved that any hero should come to the land boasting that he could do what no one among the Danes could do. He said scornfully to Beowulf—

"Tell me, art thou the Beowulf whom Breca overcame in a swimming match? I heard the tale. You both ventured out like foolish men among the waves in the days of winter. For seven nights you swam together, but Breca was the stronger. Thou wilt have a worse defeat shouldst thou venture to meet Grendel in the darkness of the night."

Beowulf answered and said, "Hunferth, my friend, thou hast drunken too much beer. Breca never overcame me in swimming, nor did any one. But if thou wouldst hear the tale, thou shalt have it. Breca and I were boys at the time, and we swam out on the wintry sea with naked swords in our hands to defend ourselves against the sea monsters. For five nights we were together upon the waves, and he could not pass me. The cold north wind blew, and there came a great storm upon the sea, and we were parted. In the darkness there came up from the bottom of the sea one of the monsters that dwell there, and it seized me and dragged me down into the deep waters. The coat of mail which I wore protected me, and I stabbed the wretch with my sword. But a great multitude of other sea monsters set upon me while I was at the bottom of the sea. I stabbed them all with my sword. When it became morning, and the sun rose, they were all washed ashore by the waves, and lay dead upon the sands. My sword had put them to sleep. Never afterwards did they hinder the sailors on their course. Afterwards I continued my journey although I was wearied, and at length the waves cast me upon the land of the Finns. I never heard that thou didst deeds such as these, Hunferth, nor Breca either. Thou didst slay thy own brothers, I know, for which thou shalt suffer the vengeance of Heaven. Hadst thou been such a hero as thou vauntest thyself, Grendel would not have laid waste the hall of thy Lord. But I, a Geat, will soon show what a brave man can do, and all men will sit down cheerfully to the mead-benches in this hall when they hear that Grendel is dead."

•••

That night, Beowulf fulfills his promise; he fights Grendel and fatally wounds him. And he has proof to back up his words; having torn off Grendel's arm in the midst of their combat, he hangs the monster's severed limb from the rafters.

•••

In the morning … it was told to Hrothgar what had taken place, and he went into the hall. He lifted up his eyes towards the high golden roof, and behold, as a trophy of the fight, there hung the arm of Grendel.

The King was glad, and he said to Beowulf, "Thou hast done a deed which all the might and wisdom of man was not able to accomplish. The mother who bore thee may well be proud of thee, Beowulf. Best of men, I love thee as my son. Ask what thou wilt of me, and I will give it. There is nothing I am not willing to give thee."

Beowulf replied, "Willingly have I served thee in this matter, O King. Would that I had been able to hinder Grendel from going away! But the wretch will not live much longer. Pain will hold him in its deadly grasp until he dies in his den. It is the doom which the pure Creator has appointed for him on account of his crimes."

All looked with wonder upon the hand of Grendel aloft upon the roof. The nails on the fingers were hard as steel. Hunferth, the son of Ecglaf, was silent as he gazed on that hand.

A Generation of Young Men Who Did What Had to Be Done

FROM *WE WHO ARE ALIVE AND REMAIN:*
UNTOLD STORIES FROM THE BAND OF BROTHERS, 2009
By Marcus Brotherton

• •

The men of Easy Company were a highly elite group; they made it through the demanding training of Camp Toccoa, parachuted into Normandy for D-Day and Holland for Operation Market Garden, fought the Germans and the freezing cold in the Battle of the Bulge, liberated concentration camps, and secured the Eagle's Nest, Hitler's mountaintop retreat.

But these men never bragged about their service; some didn't even tell their families about what they had done in the war. Men of honor don't do the courageous thing for the accolades, but because it is the right thing to do, because it is their duty.

• •

CLANCY LYALL

Today I often speak to students in schools. The number-one question I get asked is, "Did you kill anyone?" My answer is, "Yes, it was war, and I know I did. But there's more to the story that you need to know."

Were we heroes? There's no such thing as a live hero. Damn good soldiers, yes, but heroes, no. You do your job and everybody does it with you.

EARL McCLUNG

Our heroes are over there where the white crosses are. We're survivors over here. None of us are heroes. I don't think you'll talk to a man who says we are. You figure a hero is someone who does above and beyond the call of duty, and when you give your life that's as above and beyond as you can get.

ED JOINT

People come up to you and say you're a hero. I can't claim to that. "I was just an ordinary soldier with a bunch of good guys." That's all I can say about that.

JOE LESNIEWSKI

Being a hero? I don't even care for the word. I'm an individual that had a job to do. I don't feel that I'm any kind of hero. I'm just an ordinary guy like I'm supposed to be. To me, the work had to be done. I was asked to do it. So I did. When I lecture kids I tell them the same thing: don't brag that you're anything more than you are.

ED TIPPER

When I was a teenager I took freedom for granted until I got through the army and saw what the Nazis had done in Germany. Then I realized that freedom isn't automatic; it has a price.

World War II was a justified and necessary war. Last year I met five survivors of Auschwitz concentration camp. The things that happened to those people should never have happened to any human being.

Do I think my actions in the war were heroic? No, I don't. I'm even uncomfortable with the word. I was part of a generation of young men who did what had to be done.

Glory
FROM *HÁVAMÁL*
Translated by W.H. Auden and P.B. Taylor

Over 1,000 years old, the Hávamál (literally "Sayings of the High One") is a collection of Old Norse poems. Its words of wisdom provided spiritual sustenance

to the mighty Vikings, who believed the poems to be the advice of Odin, chief of the Norse gods, on how mortals should live.

....

Cattle die, kindred die,
Every man is mortal:
But the good name never dies
Of one who has done well.

Cattle die, kindred die,
Every man is mortal:
But I know one thing that never dies,
The glory of the great dead.

"Honor is the reward of virtue." —Cicero

The Soul of Honor

HONOR: AN ADDRESS TO THE CADETS OF NORWICH UNIVERSITY, AT NORTHFIELD, VERMONT ON THE COMMENCEMENT DAY, JULY 13, 1871
By Malcolm Douglass

I do not use the word Honor here in its very common sense of high reputation, or power; for men are sometimes *honored* by their fellow men, for their riches, or success, or station, or influence, who know very little of what true honor is. I do not mean that honor which one lad may obtain amongst his fellows by his superior strength, or his talents, his memory, his wit, his symmetry, or his agility. He may obtain a *kind* of honor for these things, and yet be a mean-spirited fellow after all. These accomplishments and gifts I have no fault to find with; they are good and most desirable in themselves; they are not to be despised if they are not obtained by unworthy means, and employed upon unworthy objects They may justly procure approbation for their possessor; they may often worthily attract the admiration of others; they may excite remark and criticism; they may call forth sentiments of esteem and respect from the generous, and of envy from the base. Nevertheless, the honorable notice which they bring does not necessarily secure their possessor from a great lack of true nobility of spirit. We sometimes find both gifts and a noble spirit in the same person, but the presence of the one does not guaranty the presence of the other.

This Honor, then, the honor of circumstance, of position, of power, is not that of which I would now speak. There is another species of honor, within reach of all—a higher grade; the honor of self-respect; the inner spirit and soul of honor; the honor of *thinking* good and noble thoughts; the honor of *acting* upon just, wise, and healthy principles; the honor of *living* amongst your fellows with kind and just and true and reverent regards and sympathies. The honor which frees you from meanness, vulgarity, baseness, and ignoble conceits and plans. *This* is the honor which I would now and always commend to you. It is not always popular. I do not care, or wish you to care, whether it is popular or not. I would present it for *its own* sake, and in its own simple and severe majesty. ... this honor of which I speak, and which I commend, may be sought for and gained by every one of you. This *spirit* of honor, this *self-respect*, which aims to secure, not so much the approbation of others—though it *will* secure it in a measure—as the respect and approbation of your own better nature, your own true, honest, unprejudiced, *self*.

Having said thus much, let me remind you of some of the prominent *characteristics* of this Honor.

The first characteristic which I would mention is Truth. By this I would be understood to mean both the sentiment of Truth, implanted in your nature and growing with your growth, and also its outward demonstrations; as truth of purpose, which you call Ingenuousness—truth of action, which you call Honesty—truth of speech, which you call Veracity—truth of manners, which you call Candor—truth of life, which you call Integrity—truth of principle, which you call Uprightness.

Be true then to your word; be true to your promises; be true to your instructors; be true to your fellow students; be true to *yourselves;* and be true to your God.

There is another important characteristic of true Honor, which I would next place before you. It is Fidelity. Fidelity to the trusts committed to you. I ask you to notice that old English word, Trust-worthy, i.e. worthy of confidence. It is used to point out anyone who can be depended upon to keep that securely which has been committed to him, or to discharge to the best of his ability *that* which it is his *duty* to do. Fidelity is the *soul* of trustworthiness. It is loyalty to that position in which God has placed you, and to the various trusts which are committed to you. It is a most noble characteristic.

A third characteristic of true honor is Courtesy. This is a word that includes within its meaning, Politeness, Civility, and Good Manners. I do not speak here of Etiquette, which comprehends rather the *rules* of society and of social life; rules which may greatly vary in different times and in different places, and which are easily learned if one is disposed to learn them and finds it necessary. But I speak of that which is the soul of Etiquette, which supplies it with meaning, whatever the rule of society may be; that which gives luster to civility, that which gives heart to politeness, that which gives charm to good manners. Courtesy, is a kindly desire and a considerate effort for the comfort and happiness of those around you. It is immeasurably beyond mere mannerism. It is a specific antidote to selfishness. It is a precise fulfillment, in your manners, in your words, in your gestures, of the golden rule, "Whatsoever Ye Would That Men Should

Do To You, Do Ye Even So To Them." It teaches you to place yourself, in thought, in the position of those around you; and to recognize their just claims to attention and respect. ... It teaches you, if you have hastily or thoughtlessly given pain to another, to break through the false shame and evil pride which would prevent you from acknowledging and remedying your fault. It teaches you to sympathize in some sort with the lives of your fellow beings, and to lend them a helping hand in the time of need. It develops your charity, of thought, word, and action.

Aim to be true gentlemen, to be *young* gentlemen. We do not desire you to be other than you are. We do not wish you to wear a mask, to conceal under a polished exterior the inner selfishness, vanity, malice, and rage of the heart. But in this respect to study Truth, and not only to be what you seem to be, but to be what you *ought* to seem to be—Courteous.

But I pass on to another point. If you would cherish in yourselves true Honor and self-respect, cultivate also the spirit of Reverence: Reverence for all persons and all things which are to be reverenced. Your Parents are to be reverenced ... The guardians and keepers of the Nation's power and liberties are to be reverenced, whatever their political views may be. ... Our people, old and young, greatly need reformation on this point. One of the evil fruits of the intoxication of politics which is rife amongst us, is a most disrespectful and slanderous way of dealing with the prominent men who differ from ourselves in political views, and who may be actually discharging in good faith the duties which have been committed to them by the vote of the majority of the people, according to our republican system and principles. This license in abusing the characters of our public men, because they differ from us in views of political statesmanship ... is most dishonorable. ... We may be as decided as we choose upon political theories and principles, but we must reverence the Ruler for the office's sake. ... Those who grant honor where honor is due, will not fail in their turn to receive it.

The last point which I shall venture to present to you in this list of the characteristics of true honor, is Modesty. ... In conversation, rather inquire

CHAPTER SEVEN

than declaim, rather follow than lead; or, if your duty and position calls you to lead, then strive to draw out others rather than to make a display of yourself. In setting forth your own capacities and merits, rather obtain the endorsement of others whose judgments and opinions are worthy of respect, than take pains to assert *your own* opinion of your worth. In your intercourse with others, and especially with those of the opposite sex, be respectful, be courteous, be pure-minded, be pure worded, be deferential. Do not be tempted under any circumstances, or upon any occasion, to give up a certain amount of quiet reserve, into which you will permit no one whatever to intrude. This is absolutely necessary if you would secure your own self-respect, and the thorough respect of others.

You are growing up to live, and move, and act, in the world of men, to be Citizens of this or some similar community; and the sense of true Honor which you manifest in your youth will cling round you, and ennoble and dignify you in your age. With greater and greater earnestness, then, avoid and forsake all that is low, base, mean, unworthy, and depraved, and follow the right and the true way; aiming to set in yourselves an example of the beautiful union of these grand constituents of true manly Honor: Truth; Fidelity; Courtesy; Reverence; Modesty.

AFTERWORD

Now that you've reached the end of this book, you're hopefully feeling strengthened, invigorated and inspired to live the seven manly virtues.

But you may also be feeling a bit discouraged. Perhaps the standard of manliness laid out in these chapters seems impossibly high—an ideal that can never be reached.

It probably is. And thus our cynical world would tell you, "Why bother?"

This is why cynicism is the cancer of manhood, the disease that has sapped our virility and eaten away at our *thumos*.

If you set your ideals high, while you may never reach the peak you're aiming for, you will assuredly go much farther than if you had fixed your sights on low hanging fruit or upon nothing at all. Not only will you climb higher, you will find your manhood along the way. The blood, sweat and tears you shed as you struggle toward that difficult peak will transform you into the man you wish to be. The reward is not in the destination, but in the *striving*.

This is a truth the great men you have met within these pages knew well. For example, while Benjamin Franklin never attained the "moral perfection" he sought in living a life of virtue, he believed he was "a better and a happier man" than he would have been if he had not made the attempt.

Becoming a man is not a one time event; it is a decision you make each and every day. It is a decision to rebel against society's low expectations for men. It is a challenge to not accept a life of apathy and mediocrity and to seek to become the very best man you can be. It's a decision to take the hard way, to take the path of virtue, honor and excellence, and to leave behind a lasting legacy. At its core, manliness is the decision to simply *try* and to keep on *trying*. To stand with Teddy in the arena, to fall and to get up, and to never become one of those "cold and timid souls who neither know victory nor defeat."

The voices of the great men of the past rise from the dust, hearkening to you to join them in this legacy of manliness. Will you answer the call?

PERMISSIONS

CHAPTER 1: MANLINESS

Manliness Is Teachable: From EURIPIDES, COMPLETE GREEK TRAGEDIES, EURIPIDES IV. "The Suppliant Women" trans by FW Jones. Copyright © 1959. Reprinted by permission of The University of Chicago Press.

CHAPTER 2: COURAGE

Why Direct Action?: From "Letter From Birmingham Jail." Reprinted by arrangement with The Heirs to the Estate of Martin Luther King Jr., c/o Writers House as agent for the proprietor. New York, NY.
   Copyright 1963. Dr. Martin Luther King Jr; copyright renewed 1991 by Coretta Scott King.

Duty, Honor, Country: Reprinted with permission of the General Douglas MacArthur Foundation, Norfolk, Virginia.

CHAPTER 4: RESOLUTION

Winston Churchill's Speeches During the Fall of France: Reproduced with permission of Curtis Brown Ltd, London on behalf of the Estate of Sir Winston Churchill. Copyright ©Winston S. Churchill.

Engraving of Winston Churchill: Courtesy of Berryhill & Sturgeon, Ltd.

Determination Is the Answer: From "Frozen Hell-Clancy Lyall," "Frozen Hell-Herb Suerth Jr.," "Frozen Hell-Bill Wingett," from WE WHO ARE ALIVE AND REMAIN: UNTOLD STORIES FROM THE BAND OF BROTHERS by Marcus Brotherton, copyright © 2009 by Marcus Brotherton. Used by permission of Berkley Publishing Group, a division of Penguin Group (USA) Inc.

To Fight It to the Last. The Final Letter of Robert Falcon Scott to His Wife From the South Pole: Permission granted by arrangement with Falcon Scott. Holder of the document: Scott Polar Research Institute MS 1835; BJ.

The Last of the Human Freedoms—to Choose One's Own Way: From *Man's Search for Meaning* by Viktor E. Frankl. Copyright © 1959, 1962, 1984, 1992 by Viktor E. Frankl. Reprinted by permission of Beacon Press, Boston. In the UK and Commonwealth, excluding Canada: MAN'S SEARCH FOR MEANING: THE CLASSIC TRIBUTE TO HOPE FROM THE HOLOCAUST by Viktor Frankl, published by Rider. Reprinted by permission of the Random House Group Ltd.

CHAPTER 5: SELF-RELIANCE

Our Job Was to Do Whatever We Could Do: From "Fighting in Normandy-Ed Pepping" from WE WHO ARE ALIVE AND REMAIN: UNTOLD STORIES FROM THE BAND OF BROTHERS by Marcus Brotherton, copyright © 2009 by Marcus Brotherton. Used by permission of Berkley Publishing Group, a division of Penguin Group (USA) Inc.

CHAPTER 6: DISCIPLINE

Quote from WAR by Sebastian Junger. Published by Grand Central Publishing. Used with permission of Hachette Book Group, Inc.

CHAPTER 7: HONOR

A Letter from George Washington to His Wife: Reprinted by permission of TUDOR PLACE HISTORIC HOUSE AND GARDEN, WASHINGTON, D.C.

A Generation of Young Men Who Did What Had to Be Done: From "Thoughts on Heroism" from WE WHO ARE ALIVE AND REMAIN: UNTOLD STORIES FROM THE BAND OF BROTHERS by Marcus Brotherton, copyright © 2009 by Marcus Brotherton. Used by permission of Berkley Publishing Group, a division of Penguin Group (USA) Inc.

INDEX